Marriage Miracle
15 *In* Seconds or *Less*!

*** A 100% Love Approach ***

Dr. Joseph Racite

(Author of, *The Perfect Marriage*)

Marriage Miracle
In
15 Seconds or *Less*!

*** A 100% Love Approach ***

Dr. Joseph Racite

Order this book online at www.trafford.com
or email orders@trafford.com

Most Trafford titles are also available at major online book retailers.

Printed in Victoria, BC, Canada.

ISBN: 978-1-4269-2843-7

*Our mission is to efficiently provide the world's finest, most comprehensive book publishing
service, enabling every author to experience success. To find out how to publish your book, your
way, and have it available worldwide, visit us online at www.trafford.com*

Trafford rev. 3/3/2010

Trafford
PUBLISHING® www.trafford.com

North America & international
toll-free: 1 888 232 4444 (USA & Canada)
phone: 250 383 6864 ♦ fax: 812 355 4082

To Frank and Lois

whose love, friendship and faith in me

inspired the writing of this book

THE PERFECT MARRIAGE IS ONE
IN WHICH BOTH SPOUSES
DELIBERATELY, PURPOSEFULLY,
FAITHFULLY, AND CONSISTENTLY,
IN ACTION AND SPIRIT,
PUT THEIR MARITAL VOWS AND GOD'S
DIVINE STATUTUES INTO APPLICATION
WHICH, IN TURN,
RESULTS IN MUTUAL MARITAL
SATISFACTION AND HAPPINESS.

Dr. Joseph Racite
The Perfect Marriage (1999)

Acknowledgements

It was not too long ago that my wife, Mary, and I had the privilege of being invited to our good friends, Frank and Lois, whose home is in Virginia Beach.

In the midst of one of our conversations, Frank said, *Dr. Joe, you saved my marriage and eliminated all conflict between my wife and I by one simple recommendation that you gave us and we followed.*

What was that recommendation? I asked with great curiosity.

Frank responded, *It was the recommendation you gave Lois and I regarding the 15 Second Rule: Each of us should say what we have to say and make our needs known to each other in 15 seconds or less and then make a commitment to meet them.*

Frank continued by saying, *So you should write a book that guides couples in eliminating conflict in their marriages and having the best marriage possible, as you have done for us. I mean it; I want you to write this book. Make it short and to the point so couples will not have any excuses for not reading the entire book.*

Well, Frank, your inspiration and Lois's as well, has indeed prompted me to follow your recommendation. Faith is a powerful thing. Your faith in me made this undertaking irresistible to disregard. I now have another book that contains my strongly held views regarding the keys to a mutually-fulfilling marriage. Not only will couples be able to benefit from applying the *15 Second Rule* to their marriage; they will be able to literally transform their entire marriage in 15 seconds or less, which is nothing short of a miracle.

No doubt that God's hand was in the writing of this book, as well.

I would also like to acknowledge the sacrifices that my wife, Mary, has made as I labored in completing this book during opportunities for us to have a greater amount of marital quality time than we already enjoy together. I am also indebted to my wife for her editing and constructive feedback that I solicited from her and she graciously and sacrificially gave as I wrote each chapter.

My special thanks to my youngest daughter, Lauren, who edited the entire book and offered her insights and opinions. In response to my request for constructive input, she ongoingly reminded me of the importance of balancing the recommendations given to husbands and wives.

Lastly, my thanks and gratitude always goes to God who I believe has anointed me with wisdom and understanding regarding what makes marital relationships the best they can possibly be and perfect in His eyes.

To every marriage that is transformed, I humbly give God all of the credit.

I also take very seriously the trust that has been given to me, in terms of saving marriages from divorce and teaching couples how to love to the fullest degree possible.

Contents

Introduction

Do you believe in miracles?

If you don't, this book is designed to make you a true believer – a believer in the power of love to literally transform your spouse and your marriage.

In what timeframe?

15 seconds or less!

The word, *transform*, has several definitions. Within the context and premise of this book, it means, *to change the condition and nature of your marriage to all it can be.*

The ingredient and power for this transformation process is 100% love.

The end result of this transformation is your miracle, *the perfect marriage.*

This book indeed delivers the promise of its message; that is, *the perfect marriage* is possible to every married couple that puts love into practice on a moment-by-moment basis. This requires each spouse to say, do, and give of themselves what is necessary to meet the other spouse's stated marital needs completely and to make him or her as happy as possible.

Why would less than 100% love be the standard for attaining a happy and healthy relationship for any marriage?

This book has been written out of necessity, due to the fact that most married couples are being misled by well-intentioned authors and professionals, including the clergy, who are advocating and promoting principles and approaches that do not conform to and, in fact, divert from the letter and spirit of the marital vows, including the vow, *to love.*

Teaching couples how to engage in fair fighting, never-ending reflective listening, or learning to put on a big, happy smiley face, in response to a selfish and withholding spouse who refuses to change, are but a few examples of why couples are often in a danger zone, even after they have successfully completed their couple's counseling.

The end result of unmet marital needs, arising from non-love-oriented recommendations, is unprecedented infidelity, ongoing marital conflict on a regular basis in nearly every married home, co-existent marriages, and an unacceptable divorce rate.

The true victims arising from these problems are the children, who are subjected to dysfunctional and unhappy home environments with parents who are *in the dark*, with respect to resolving their marital issues and moving forward in a way that leads to a mutually happy and fulfilled marriage that, in turn, benefits the whole family.

I have read most of the best-selling books that have been written on marriage; however, universal standards are omitted that provide love-based standards and answers and place the same yardstick of responsibility upon both spouses in the marriage. The bona-fide truth regarding what makes marriages work has been replaced with watered-down and distorted versions of love, designed to cater to the violator of them.

In short, the actual practice of love has been replaced by the subjective feelings of the violator of love. Thus, whoever makes the best case of being the victim in the therapeutic setting, becomes the winner in the marital struggle and recipient of the changes that are imposed on the other spouse, the villain. Thus, the responsibility for making the changes required for rebuilding the marriage from its' war-torn state rests predominately on "the accused," as opposed to both spouses.

Unfortunately, all too often, therapists are required to bite their tongue and "walk on eggshells," least the perceived victim go immediately to his or her divorce attorney right after the session.

To make matters worse, in reality, the courts award divorce simply for the asking and then award the true villain, such as one who simply won't try to make the necessary changes, an equal distribution of assets and, quite often, custody of the children and lifetime alimony.

The success or failure of the institution of marriage rests upon the adherence of the marriage vows.

When was the last time you read a book on marriage that defined and explained these vows, while placing complete responsibility upon each spouse in unconditionally meeting them to the fullest extent?

The act of marriage is a spiritual and legal act, both of which bind spouses together by the act of their will. While the letter and spirit of the marital vows stipulate the obligations of each spouse to one another, these obligations are only bound in heaven.

Here on planet Earth, the definition of marriage, along with the expectations that are associated with completely fulfilling the obligations associated with marriage, have become very distorted and redefined to a point that very few have a realistic ideas of what they truly are.

And no one is willing to step up to the plate, figuratively speaking, to point out what these obligations are and to place blame where it truly belongs.

One of the main purposes of this book is to do just that!

The embodiment of all of the marital vows can be contained in one word – love. But what does this word really mean, what forms does it take, and what is the ultimate goal of love? The answers to these questions are contained in this straightforward book in straight-talk fashion.

Unfortunately, most books are written in a style that caters to the Reader and/or the publisher. The warm and fuzzy presentations and explanations that are provided in the typical book on marriage give the Reader some direction in a general sense, but fall short of providing absolutes, the complete truth and, thus, real answers. As such, this book does not fall short of providing the absolute standard of love to every conceivable hair-splitting marital issue and conflict.

In addition, shortcomings are highlighted of the various approaches, misapplied principles, and fallacies that have resulted in couples asking for directions from marriage counseling professionals, in hopes of enabling them to reach their intended destination of marital bliss, only to find themselves stuck in a marital wilderness state, unhappy, unfulfilled, frustrated and directionless.

In addition, the fundamental and underlying issues that couples struggle with are not addressed in most approaches to resolving marital discord. Rather, the couple's marital symptoms, such as "poor communication," are highlighted as the primary problem for intervention. Wouldn't you agree that the wind behind the sails is what drives the boat? In this analogy, the wind represents the unseen and unknown forces that push the marriage in a certain direction. Wrong approaches push the marriage in the wrong direction.

What is most alarming is that these forces are not typically known to struggling couples, because they are not typically identified. In the illustration, as previously stated, the boat represents the spouse who is being blamed for the marriage being ship-wrecked. Wouldn't you agree that going in the right direction would have circumvented a ship-wreck?

This book makes the case that love-in-action must be the driving force in every marriage.

Anything less than 100% love in practice involves the effects of fear that takes the form of defensiveness and self-centeredness.

Once spouses make a 15-second decision to shift their thinking and behavior to conform to a love mindset, the couple will be well on their way to their desired marital destination - mutual marital happiness and satisfaction. This will require them to, as explained throughout most of the chapters herein, to shift their thinking *from the get to the give*, and to disregard much of the past instruction they have received regarding putting love into practice in their marriage.

You will, for the first time ever, read recommendations that are not found in other books which, in fact, will put married couples on the right course. For example, you will read that spouses are entitled to get all of their marital needs met unconditionally and that the receiver determines whether and when these needs are met.

Contracts entitle individuals to the specified rights that have been agreed-upon. The marital vows form the basis of receiving the entitlement of love. During the wedding ceremony both vow, *to love*, at the marriage alter.

While motivating one's spouse through exhibiting loving behaviors is advocated, the Reader is instructed to embrace commitment, which requires putting love into practice when he or she has little or no motivation for meeting them. The basis for unconditional marital commitment is likewise rooted in the marital vows that were exchanged that entitle each spouse to 100% from the other, such as marital fidelity, but also lays forth the mutual responsibilities to be fulfilled by each spouse. Picking and choosing the particular vows that will be honored 100% is depicted as a "cafeteria-style" marriage.

The recommendations made throughout this book are rooted in research, my professional training and experience, and my findings over a span of 33 years of professional practice in the field of mental health and marriage & family therapy.

At times, I borrow principles, illustrations, and recommendations from my previous book, *The Perfect Marriage*.

In addition, at times, Bible-based quotes, references, and inferences are made to drive home my irrefutable points that can be put-to-the-test with the results that I predict. Given the fact that marriage is a spiritual act, any professional and author would be in error to not reference the religious connotations and denotations of marriage for consideration.

Unlike any other book that you will read on marriage, the straight-talk tone of my message is as direct as are my recommendations, and I do not fall short of confronting the Reader about his or her fear, selfishness, and ignorance of the facts. My purpose for doing this is to wake the Reader up and challenge him or her to do exactly what I recommend and reap the results that are promised – that is, a marriage miracle.

In fact, this book contains some exercises that will indeed lead the Reader to the same conclusions that conform to the core message of this book, while successfully refuting the falsehoods that have been promoted for decades and destroyed countless number of marriages.

While the human body requires oxygen, minerals, nutrients, water, and food to survive, a marriage likewise requires certain things to survive and be healthy as well. This book instructs couples regarding what is needed for a marriage to be healthy and for both spouses to be exceedingly happy and fulfilled, such as sufficient marital quality time, with an emphasis on each spouse reaching out to meet each other's gender-specific marital needs. Individual chapters are devoted to the wife and to the husband in the form of an instruction manual. The final chapter provides a systematic approach to married couples for implementing the specific recommendations contained throughout the book.

It is intended for the Reader to find it irresistible to forsake not making all of the changes that are recommended for his or her marriage miracle. Numerous examples are provided throughout this book that literally make the case that the marriage miracle transformation process is but 15 seconds of less from becoming a reality.

For those who chose to put 100% love consistently into practice in his or her marriage, abundant marital blessings undeniably lie ahead.

In the same way that one would not expect anyone to run the marathon with a broken leg, there are some exceptions to which the principles of this book applies, such as with individuals with a severe mental illness or medical conditions, those with deeply engrained personality or characterological disorders, and those who are addicted to or regularly abuse alcohol or drugs. Hopefully, any spouse, who is resistant to forsaking his or her selfish withholding, will not attempt to diagnose his or her spouse as having a

BiPolar Disorder. Using diagnostic characterizations is a very common tactic being used today as a loophole for not being accountable, making the necessary changes, or engaging one-hundred percent in the marital counseling process.

My deepest wish is for every couple to attain their "marriage miracle." Thus, my very straightforward and confrontive approach is not designed to be offensive but, rather, to reach you, with the hopes of alerting you of the misconceptions that you embrace which are at the heart of why you have not realized the marriage of your dreams.

If attaining a miracle in your marriage was not possible, I would have not written this book.

Moreover, this proven approach will deliver the promise of the title of this book if you do exactly what is recommended and not resort to old behaviors that have not resulted in your attaining a mutually happy and fulfilling marriage.

Lastly, if it were not for the gratitude of my friends, Frank and Lois, in response to their "marriage miracle," coupled with their insistence that I write this book, perhaps many who now have the opportunity to read it and attain *the perfect marriage* would have, figuratively speaking, otherwise remained stuck somewhere in the Arctic, believing that they were en route to sunny-side Florida.

Therefore, I urge you to follow my directives, and prepare for your marriage miracle.

Yes, in 15 seconds or less!

CHAPTER 1

Foundation for Your Marriage Miracle

A marriage miracle in 15 seconds or less?

Perhaps you may be wondering whether the word *miracle* refers to an actual miracle that will occur from a direct intervention from God. Certainly miracles often become manifest instantaneously. Therefore, you may be also wondering whether this book is about religion or, perhaps, if it tells a story of a distressed married couple whose marriage was on the brink of divorce wherein, suddenly, in 15 seconds or less, something miraculous happened that changed their marriage forever.

Well, to those of you who trust God at His word, you will certainly see something seemingly divine become manifest as you read about the principles herein that will literally change your marriage in practically an instant ... or, better said, *15 seconds or less!*

The Importance of 100% Love

The scoffers and skeptics won't see anything but roadblocks to overcoming their marital obstacles because they are blinded and immobilized by their refusal to put into practice what is recommended that throughout this book – authentic love.

By love, I am not referring to a fuzzy feeling, nor am I referring to simply being kind. I am explicitly referring to the actual practice of giving of yourself with heart, unconditionally and completely, with the single-minded intention and acting in a way that ultimately achieves the goal of meeting all of your spouse's marital needs and, in doing so, making him or her as happy as possible.

Individuals who are blinded, misguided, fearful, self-focused, narcissistic, and/or immobilized, experience real difficulty putting love into actual practice and, when they do so, each step taken is reluctantly and with caution so as to minimize the potential threat that they perceive lies ahead, such as being hurt, used, shortchanged, inconvenienced, taken advantage of, or over-controlled.

Which of these potential threats do you identify with, in consideration of the idea of giving of yourself unconditionally and completely to make your spouse completely happy?

How do you feel about putting love into 100% practice in your relationship or marriage through your giving of yourself?

Anything less than 100% love is giving combined with withholding; a recipe resulting in a mathematical certainty for a problematic marriage.

If asked, what would your spouse say that you fall short of meeting which would make him or her completely happy and fulfilled in your marriage 100% of the time? Affection? Sex? Connecting communication? Quality time? Trustworthiness? Forgiveness? Spiritual growth?

Perhaps you believe that you already practice 100% love and, for this reason, what you are about to read is yet another book that conveys the same old message you've heard before.

To the contrary, this is a new win-win approach based putting 100% love into practice that, in turn, provides solutions to every conceivable issue regarding marriage. Moreover, systematic steps and fail-proof marital principles are provided for you to attain them, while maximizing a loving response from your spouse and transforming your marriage forever.

How long should your marriage miracle take if you follow my directives?

You guessed it – 15 seconds or less!

Why 15 Seconds or Less?

As I was writing this book, my wife commented, *I don't understand what the 15 seconds is all about!*

My reply was, *It would probably be more accurate to replace the words 15 seconds or less with the word, "instantaneous." However, one of the main reasons why I have decided to write this book is because one particular recommendation that I gave to a couple, Frank and Lois, involving a 15 second limit on them each presenting their feelings and points of view to each other, literally saved their marriage. And it was this couple that practically insisted that I write this book.*

Therefore, the words *15 seconds or less* can be interchangeably used with the words *instant* or *instantaneous,* regarding the marital transformation that lies quickly ahead.

Whether it be instantaneous or within the time frame of 15 seconds or less, as you put into practice the principles and simple recommendations that are provided, you will indeed be on the road that delivers the promise of your marriage miracle.

The word *miracle* refers to a remarkable event that occurs in your marriage. However, you may also come to believe, as Frank and Lois did, that God was the guiding and driving force in terms of them receiving an answer to their prayers, a bona-fide marriage miracle.

To The Skeptics Who Are Still in The Dark

The examples, illustrations, and stories I use throughout this book are designed to make skeptics into believers. If you live your life according to the motto, *seeing is believing,* then I believe that you will not be disappointed. I hope to convince you to change your thinking from the culturally-driven status quo, by making the case why you should forsake your old and useless approaches for eliminating your marital distress and, instead, attaining a very happy marriage.

The outcome of putting love into actual practice will be a mutually fulfilling marriage to those who simply apply the principles and concrete recommendations contained herein, instead of using their well-intentioned approaches. Thus, your *perfect marriage* is at hand.

Please consider the fact that a half-truth is still not the truth. In fact, 99% of the truth is also not the truth. Would you consider your spouse as faithful if he or she was faithful 99% of the time? I am sure that you would not. Therefore, anything less than 100% is unacceptable.

With this in mind, it is essential that you not preferentially pick and choose the principles and recommendations that you feel like applying but, rather, apply 100% of them. In short, you are simply being asked to put 100% love into practice in your marriage on a moment-to-moment basis. If you do, you will get back a 100% return and have "the perfect marriage."

At this point, you may be thinking, *No one has a perfect marriage!* Attaining, *the perfect marriage*, <u>not</u> *a perfect marriage*, is the intent of this book. Would you prefer reading about yet another repackaged approach to marital happiness that has flaws or "leaks" in it? Think about the very small leaks that sunk the unsinkable ship, the *Titanic*, in a mere few hours.

Please consider that, if the leaks in the *Titanic* were large enough, it could have sunk in 15 seconds or less! While the sinking of a ship in this example refers to a negative outcome, the alternative can likewise be true. In this regard, a positive action, if large enough, can lead to the biggest positive outcome as possible – an extremely remarkable one; yes, a marriage miracle … and in 15 seconds or less! Yes, this is as exciting as it sounds!

Certainly, a universal law of physics applies; that is, *for every action, there is an equal and opposite reaction.* Some religious scholars call it *the law of attraction*; common folk simply assert that *what goes around comes around.* The Bible refers to it as *sowing and reaping.* In any case, the end result is the same; you get to the degree or proportion that you give.

When applying this principle to marriage, it is possible for any couple to have the relationship of their dreams. Likewise, they can have the worst marriage on this planet.

Be honest. Aren't you reading with the hope of attaining the best possible marriage or relationship? And aren't you tired of having to settle or in waiting for results for your efforts?

You also may be asking yourself, *When is God going to answer my prayers?* To receive your answer, are you truly willing to make the necessary changes to receive your answer?

At this point, you may be thinking to yourself, *Yeah, but I didn't cause the problem in my marriage* or *I have tried everything and nothing works!*

Perhaps everything you have tried does not work; but are you willing to do what is recommended in this book? If you aren't, then you cannot truly assert that you have.

As you continue to read, I believe that you will begin to conclude that you are a big part of the problem that does not make a 100% outcome possible in your marriage. Muscling, attempting to coerce, punishing, or threatening your spouse into embracing your template, construct, or points-of-view of achieving marital happiness will not work either. In fact, these types of behaviors are indicative of behaviors that are the antithesis of what is being recommended. Putting love into action *through giving* in your marriage is what is strictly recommended; as such, the changes you desire in your spouse depend upon you changing.

For your loving actions, through giving, to have a transforming effect, you must stop saying and doing those things that put a wedge between you and your spouse, along with the need to stop blaming your spouse for your unloving actions. You must also stop withholding from your spouse. Withholding is analogous to wanting a harvest without planting a seed.

In addition, withholding is the antithesis of giving. Love always takes the form of giving. Therefore, if you are not giving, you are not being loving. Coming up with reasons for your withholding, when you truly have the ability to give, is analogous to adding insult to injury.

Regarding the issue of 15 seconds or less, I am equally certain that it would be your hope that, if possible, you could have "the perfect marriage" within that timeframe. In my view, this certainly is not an unreasonable desire. In fact, if you want anything less, why continue reading? And why continue to complain about your spouse and your marriage?

Think about all of the things that you do in life with minimal effort, expecting or, at least hoping for, a certain and almost immediate result. For example, how often do you simply push a button and expect a result in 15 seconds or less? When you turn the key in your car, don't you expect the car to start in 15 seconds or less? When you push the light switch up or down, don't you expect the light to turn on or off in 15 seconds or less? And wouldn't you agree that it is reasonable to expect almost immediate results when you do these things? Also, please consider the fact that most people do not give it any thought as to whether their car will start when they simply turn the key. Why? Because they trust in the electrical principles that underlie the end result of what they indeed expect – a car that starts instantaneously with the simple turning of the key.

If your car did not start, wouldn't it be reasonable to conclude that something fundamental is wrong and that it needs to be repaired? Hopefully, you would be willing to bring your car to a mechanic that would know how to repair it.

In applying this illustration to your marriage, have you talked to professionals or read books on the topic of marriage that provide answers to not only make your marriage better but to fix it? Is your marriage fixed? If not, why? What's creating the delay?

Have you been advised that it will take weeks, months, or years to fix your marriage?

What would you say to a mechanic who informed you that it would take weeks, months, or perhaps years to fix your car?

How would you like it if it took more than 15 seconds for your car to start?

Are you beginning to understand what I am trying to convey?

Also consider the fact that your car cannot fix itself. Your marriage is no different. If you do nothing, your marriage will stay the same or most likely get worse. Also, if the advice you are following from a book, friend, or professional has not resulted in your marriage being dramatically transformed to one of your dreams, simply continue reading and you will discover why. Figuratively speaking, this book is designed to help you fill in those holes in your "marriage ship" that is causing it to fill up with water and ultimately sink.

The great news is that you can fix, correct, repair, and begin the complete transformation of your marriage in 15 seconds or less! And after you have completed reading this book, you will not need to hear anyone else's advice and, also, will realize that you have total control on making this transformation become a reality. Love in action trumps any advice that can be given; there is no equivalent or substitute.

And love never fails!

How long would it take you to accept one million dollars?

15 seconds or less?

The reason why you would gladly accept a gift of one million dollars is because you have *heart*. When an individual has heart, it creates a sense of urgency and prompts his or her initiative. No reminders would be required from others to pick the money up as a condition for keeping it, nor would a long and hard day at work or with the kids be an excuse used by you for not picking it up as soon as possible.

How much is your marriage worth?

I'm sure that you love your children. How much is their happiness and security worth to you?

You would lay down your life for them, right?

Then lay down all of your excuses, your pride, your prioritization of other people and things over your marriage, your need to be "one up" on your spouse and, yes, your selfishness, and, instead, choose to lay down your life by choosing to make the simple but necessary attitudinal and behavioral changes that are necessary to make your spouse as happy as possible.

Yes, make a decision to do those things that would make your spouse 100% happy, 100% of the time.

You have 15 seconds or less to decide! Okay? Are you ready?

What's the pause about?

If you paused, please be assured that your pause is not about your spouse; it's about your fear!

Fear is something that you learned long before you met your spouse. It arises out of your perception of threat, resulting in your need to defend yourself against this threat. In this regard, you become defensive, either in the form of *fight* or *taking flight*. However, these mechanisms keep you stuck.

Couples typically fight by arguing and name-calling. Taking flight occurs when a spouse does what he or she deems necessary to avoid an argument. It also takes passive-aggressive forms, resulting in the withholding of meeting the other spouse's marital needs, such as affection or sex, prioritizing work, friends or children, or in having a marital affair.

Interestingly, the research regarding marital affairs indicates that in as high as 90% of the cases, conflict avoidance is at the heart of the underlying dynamic in the marriage. The *American Association for Marriage and Family Therapy* (AAMFT) posts in its' web site that conflict avoidance is the #1 cause of divorce. [1]

Interestingly, the *New Testament* of the Bible states that, *true love casts out all fear*. Thus, fear fills in the vacuum of where love does not exist.

In his book, *Your Sacred Self*, Dr. Wayne Dyer, writes that the opposite of love is not hate; it is fear. [2]

Thus, your spouse is not the primary problem; your fear is!

Please consider that if love in practice is the answer to relationship problems, then the manifestations of fear in any form (e.g., defensiveness, unforgiveness, arguing, bringing up the past, holding grudges) cannot be exhibited by you and must cease. If you are exhibiting them, you are basically holding onto the belief that responding to your fear is the answer, yet illogically expect an automatic love response from your spouse.

If you are not afraid, then why do you defensively act or respond in such a way so as to protect yourself, attempt to *even the score* when you feel slighted or shortchanged, or not give your spouse the opportunity to take advantage or get the upper hand?

When we are afraid, we also have a tendency to be selfish and self-focused, as opposed to being focused on the marital needs for our spouses. Therefore, rather than wanting to listen to understand what we need to do to make our spouses happy, we instead want to be heard to voice our complaints and our unmet needs.

Isn't this what you often find yourself doing?

Using another illustration, if you believed that someone nearby was possibly intending to hit you, wouldn't you be in a defensive mood wherein you would be focused on how to protect yourself?

This is the disposition of couples several times a day in their marital relationship; they are in a defensive mode controlled by fear, as opposed to a love mode wherein they are guided and driven by love. Are you willing to be guided by love – yes, 100% love?

Be honest; does one day go by that you are not privately or openly upset with your spouse? If you are focused 100% on your spouse's highest good, as opposed to your own, how could you feel this way so often?

In reality, you are choosing to be upset, as opposed to choosing to love; it's that simple! And your refusal to change keeps this unhealthy and unfulfilling relational dynamic alive.

It takes two to argue. Therefore, if you are engaged in an argument, you are doing the opposite of what love requires and are therefore part of the problem in your marriage. During an argument, conflict, power struggle, spat, or fight you are focused on your highest good, not your spouse's. You are focused on what you have not been getting, as opposed to what you need to be giving.

Once again, love always takes the form of giving.

To love, you must give.

Arguing takes the love percentage from 100% to at least 99%.

Consider this – if marital needs are being completely need, what is there to argue about?

In short, poor communication or a lack of communication in your marriage is mere evidence that love is not being practiced. It is a symptom of the underlying problem but, unfortunately, is typically identified and treated as the central or primary problem by most well-meaning therapists. But it's not the real problem; practicing less than 100% love is!

In examining the issue regarding conflict avoidance (i.e., lack of communication), here is a question for you to consider with respect to marital infidelity. In this regard, do you know anyone who has had a marital affair who was getting all of his or her marital needs met before the affair started?

Come on – be totally honest.

Wouldn't you admit that at least something was missing in the marriage to bridge a true love connection?

In response to these questions, in addition to your feelings of irritation, I am certain that you began thinking that it doesn't matter whether the cheating spouse was or was not getting his or her marital needs met ... infidelity is wrong and the spouse that was cheated on was and is always entitled to faithfulness.

If this is what you are thinking, I am delighted to say that I agree with you totally!

But you are also probably thinking, *Then why did you infer that cheating spouses commit adultery in response to not getting marital needs met, as though this justifies cheating?*

Dear Reader, this supposition is yours alone.

In fact, if this is what you were thinking, you are being defensive!

In the same way that a sneeze facilitates a *God bless you* response, an unmet marital need facilitates reciprocation in some form. At times, the form that it takes is adultery. Adultery is a marital fidelity need that is not met. While, in reality, there is no legitimate excuse for it, there is likewise no legitimate excuse for meeting other marital needs that one has the ability to meet if he or she has the ability.

In consideration of the fact that approximately one-half of the couples enter counseling together, due to infidelity as the presenting problem, it becomes even more important to fortify your marriage into a 100% love-based marriage to make it affair-proof.

As one possible explanation of your defensiveness or defensive posture, could it be that you are defending against your failure or reluctance to meet all of your spouse's marital needs?

And what makes one marital need superior to the other?

What makes the refusal to have sex with your spouse less wrong because you don't feel like it, than the refusal to abide by continuous fidelity because your spouse doesn't feel like it? While our culture dictates otherwise, you must begin to accept marital needs as moral and spiritual equivalents because these two needs are both rooted in Biblical teaching and were contained within your marital vows. Right?

Unfortunately, most spouses construct a list of offenses on a vertical, as opposed to a horizontal, plane. The biggest offenses are put on top of the list, whereas their failures or shortcomings are placed at the very bottom and attached to a laundry-list of lame excuses and justifications for not meeting them.

In reality, only the deprived spouse can assign a weight to the degree of hurt that is experienced from the spouse who chooses to withhold. Do you hear what I am saying?

When you said your marital vows, unless there were contingency clauses inserted and verbally exchanged between you and your spouse-to-be, what did you mean when you said, *to love?* Was it understood and conveyed to your spouse-to-be that the, *to love,* vow meant, *if and when I feel like it, if I can find the time* or, *if and when you deserve it?*

The thinking that takes one or more of the verbal forms of *if and when I feel like it, you can't make me do anything I don't want to do, if you deserve it,* or *you're a control freak* (for wanting it) would only be used by someone who has no respect for his or her marriage vows if any of these reasons were used to justify infidelity.

Wouldn't you agree?

Yet, these justifications are used without a blink of an eye by nearly every married couple for shortchanging their spouses' other marital needs.

Are you willing to get onto the 100% love track?

And has anyone ever told you or implied that your spouse is a "control freak" for expecting his or her marital needs to be met and met 100% of the time? Once again, you expect fidelity 100% of the time whether your spouse feels like it or not or wants to. Then why do you and others impose a different standard where it comes to meeting the letter and spirit of the other marital vows?

As you can see, the problem with many well-meaning helping professionals and books written on the topic of love and marriage is in the inconsistent application of its' meaning in all aspects of the marriage. If you agree with me, you are now headed in the right direction.

Incidentally, upon discovery of your spouse cheating on you, how long would it take for you to consider divorce … 15 seconds or less?

And if we are in agreement on the issue regarding spouses being entitled to fidelity, I am almost certain that you will understand, as you read on, why your many attempts at attaining a mutually-fulfilling marriage have not worked to your satisfaction.

In the next chapter, you will begin to see and understand how, in effect, you have not been "faithful," in terms of keeping all of your marriage vows, even though you have not actually cheated on your spouse.

At this point, you may be thinking, *Who, me? I keep all of my marriage vows!*

Well, if you believe that you have kept them all, please hold that thought tightly and open your mind widely; this is the key to doing what is necessary to receive your 15 second marriage miracle!

Once you know the direction you are to take, you will truly be in the driver's seat and destined to attain, *the perfect marriage.*

While you still may be skeptic to a certain degree, please don't turn back; your marriage miracle is just ahead.

CHAPTER 2

The Right Direction for Attaining Your Marriage Miracle

Couples who come for marriage counseling do so with the ultimate goal of attaining a happy, harmonious, and mutually-fulfilling marriage.

The majority of couples entering counseling are experiencing marital conflict and unhappiness, arising from unmet marital needs, an emotional disconnection, inadequate marital quality time, or poor communication.

Fear, confusion, and despair controls the distressed couple as both spouses wrestle with a number of unresolved issues and ineffective problem-solving strategies and coping mechanisms for reducing the impact of their marital problems in a win-win scenario. However, unless infidelity has been committed, neither spouse uses the marital vows as their frame of reference, in terms of understanding the origin of their marital difficulties or the resolution of them.

In fact, approximately 99% of the couples have the tendency to spend 99% of the time focused on the marital problems and who is to blame for them, while spending 1% on the possible solutions.

Identifying problems and the one who is to blame for them solves nothing!

Nevertheless, practically every couple stuck in conflict is disgruntled regarding what each of them has not been *getting* from the other. Both feel shortchanged and victimized, causing them to struggle with feelings of frustration, distrust, anger, and hopelessness.

Are you feeling this way to any degree in your marriage?

Your Motive is Right, but Your Direction is Wrong

While couples in counseling settings certainly have the right marital goal, they are approaching it in the wrong way; that is, their approach to reaching their goals is incorrect. In fact, their tendency to do the opposite of what is needed to be on the right track for resolving their marital problems is at the core of why they find themselves stuck, in terms of resolving them.

Are you willing to take the right direction to attaining your marriage miracle?

As an illustration, I liken their wrong approach to attempting to attain mutual marital fulfillment and happiness to driving on *Interstate 95 North* to Florida from New Jersey, as opposed to *Interstate 95 South*.

In this regard, I tell them, *If either of you asked me to provide you with the best direction to drive your car to Florida from New Jersey, I would tell you to get onto Interstate 95 South after you cross over the Delaware Memorial Bridge and then stay on this route. If you do, you shall eventually, but surely, arrive to Florida.*

In this illustration, taking *Route 95 North* (from a New Jersey location) represents couples going in the wrong direction to attain mutual marital happiness and satisfaction. By the words *wrong direction*, I am referring to their wrong approach to attaining it.

What makes it the "wrong approach" is that they are focused on what they have not been *getting* from each other, as opposed to what they need to be *giving* to each other.

If a couple actually wants to go to Florida, which represents their desired destination of attaining mutual marital happiness and fulfillment, they must take *Route 95 South*, which represents putting 100% love into practice in their marriage.

Sound simple?

In effect, it really is, if you are willing to spend 15 seconds or less to what I term, *shifting your thinking from the "get" to the "give."*

Yes, it is essential that you shift, *from the get to the give!*

What do I actually mean by this?

You simply must focus exclusively on what you need to be *giving* your spouse, as opposed to what you have not been *getting* from your spouse.

Why?

Because love is the answer! And, once again, love always takes the form of giving.

The goal of love is the other person's highest good!

I know that I am sounding repetitious, but you need to hear it over and over and over; it is that important! So are you willing to make the "love shift" to head in the right direction?

Consequently, in order to put love into practice in your relationship, you always need to ask yourself (regardless of your spouse's hurtful words or actions), *What is it that I need to be saying, doing, or giving to make my spouse as happy as possible and feel loved?*

Therefore, the next time your spouse gets upset with you, instead of reacting, ask your spouse this question. Then do what is absolutely necessary to make your spouse feel loved.

Perhaps you may feel that this is a ridiculous and self-deprecating thing to do and that the thought of it makes you cringe.

Yet, if I asked you if you believed that putting love into practice is the answer you would unhesitantly agree with me … and in 15 seconds or less!

You instantly know that love is the answer. Unfortunately, in my view, you have been guided the wrong way, taught the wrong approach, and brainwashed into believing something that you actually disagree with. Thus, you walk around with an invisible banner that reads, *I not going to take his (or her) crap!* Sorry for being uncouth; but that is what your attitude conveys.

While you believe that love is the answer, it would appear that you believe that it is the answer only to the degree to which you believe you are being treated. In effect, you define love basically as a reciprocation that makes you feel a certain way, and nothing more. And then you wonder why your marriage has lost its' zest, its' vigor, its' fulfillment, and its' life.

Who, me?

Yes, you!

Perhaps you have read too many books that promote absurd and counterproductive concepts and ideas such as fair fighting, negotiating your marital needs, putting love into practice on your own terms, compromising, or communicating effectively to get what you want in your marriage.

Once again, if you are not giving, you are actually withholding.

Please consider who benefits from the withholding?

Certainly not your spouse!

Withholding keeps you and the marriage on a route away from attaining a mutually-fulfilling marriage and to a destination of marital unhappiness.

Like a poison, withholding has an insidious and lethal effect upon the marriage. But its' symptoms are noticeable, such as boredom, irritation, lack of fulfillment, feeling trapped, and depressed mood.

Thus, if something appears to be missing from your marriage, it would appear that someone is not giving what is essential for the marriage to be all it could and should.

Could that someone be you?

Do I hear a, *Yes, but …* response?

How Most Couples Get Off Track During Couple's Counseling

Unfortunately, most therapists attempt to help their clients by intervening to teach them how to communicate effectively while they are driving in the wrong direction on Route 95 North!

As time passes, marital needs are negotiated in these counseling sessions and, as a means of circumventing divorce, the alienated or selfish spouse is not confronted or pressured in any way to put into practice what love requires … which is unconditional and heartfelt giving in an effort to meet the other spouse's marital needs.

If you have been in couple's counseling before, you know exactly what I mean!

And to what degree did it truly benefit you?

You certainly wouldn't be reading this book if you did not need direction for attaining a happier and more fulfilling marriage.

Be Accountable and Examine Your Attitude

How would you assess yourself in your current situation with your spouse?

Do you get defensive at the drop of a hat?

Does your spouse seemingly avoid getting emotionally close to you?

Do you ask your spouse to be totally open and transparent and then become angry and disconnecting when it is given?

Due to how you are feeling towards your spouse, do you believe that it takes great audacity to expect you to meet every one of your spouse's marital needs?

Are you basically saying to yourself at this time, *If Dr. Racite thinks for one minute that I am going to bow down to my spouse and continue to allow myself to be mistreated or abused, he has got to be crazy?!*

If this is what you are thinking at this time, please consider this: If you assert that love is the answer and desperately want love, but then do the exact opposite of what love requires that, in turn, generates a negative response from your spouse, who is actually the crazy one – me or you?!

So let me ask you, *How do you feel about shortchanging your spouse?*

The reason why I am asking you is because your attitude to this question will certainly dictate your feelings and your actions.

Your attitude dictates your feelings and actions, not your spouse.

Are you feeling like putting this book down and looking for another book that supports your orientation of being a victim so you don't have to examine how your actions and your withholding have contributed to the marital distress and unhappiness you and your spouse are experiencing?

If you are, now is the time to be master over your fear and allow love to be in the driver's seat.

Also, how can you possibly reason that your negative attitude will generate a positive loving response from your spouse?

And, while I may be presumptuous, during any part of your reading, have you pondered at all as to whether I am crazy, irrational, rigid-minded, egotistical, out-of-this world or something like that?! If you have, this is a typical response to fear arising from being indoctrinated in this culture that claims to have the answers, but doesn't.

Please be logical; a loving action produces a loving reaction.

I am in a fighting mood to rescue from your plight in the wrong direction and feel passionate about doing it. So please understand that I need to challenge the premises of your thinking throughout your reading, and the indoctrination that it is linked to. This is sort of a Cognitive-Behavioral approach to getting you unstuck. I want to give you the truth so you will be set free.

Keep on reading; I'm doing my best to make a believer of you so you will get your marriage miracle. I know that you can do it, and I refuse to give up on you!

You must go forward and not step back. Please consider the fact that a combination of loving actions, in conjunction with a number of unloving actions, is analogous to taking two steps forward and then two steps background. And you say that you want to go to Florida?

Be honest with yourself; you have been stuck and stranded, and the only way to move forward is to *put your love in gear*! So do it … in 15 seconds or less!

Also, consider the fact that being reluctant to conform your thinking to a *love mindset* to what love requires is analogous to hitting someone in the face and then feeling disgruntled and victimized when you do not get a love response in return.

And when you do give of yourself, isn't it true that you expect your loving actions will be reciprocated in 15 seconds or less?

Try meeting your spouse's most desired or cherished marital need and *with heart* … then you can begin counting to 15.

You may also be saying to yourself at this point, *Yes, but I have tried that and it doesn't work!* My *Yes, but…* response to you is, *Have you consistently and completely met all of your spouse's marital needs to his or her specification, exhibiting an attitude of love, or have you done this in a hit-or-miss fashion and with the wrong motive of being loving so it would benefit you, as opposed to making your spouse as happy as possible? Also, has this been verified by your spouse?*

Are there other marital needs that are being ignored that undermine the impact of your efforts? For example, are you being romantic on one hand, yet become defensive when your spouse attempts to discipline the children? Do you critique your spouse or, in so many words or actions, convey your disapproval when your spouse imposes consequences on your children's misbehavior? Regarding your spouse's other needs, do you set the terms regarding how you choose to meet them or make your spouse feel ashamed, selfish, mentally warped, or guilty about any one of them?

Stop giving, *Yes, but …* answers and contemplating, *How about if …* questions. Whatever comes after the word "but" in your verbal response is your excuse for not giving and it is this excuse that is keeping the marriage stuck and stranded! Your, *How about if …* questions are most likely the inquiries you are making to find a loophole, so you don't have to meet one of your spouse's marital needs. *Dr. Racite, how about if I don't feel like …?*

How about if you begin putting 100% love into practice and then begin to see your spouse transform right before your eyes?

How about if you begin shifting your thinking *from the get to the give*?

Please keep in mind that *two become one* in every sense the moment you got married. Therefore, you must accept the proposition that you either both win together or you both lose together. In this regard, you must understand that your withholding will definitely cause you to lose if you do not make the necessary changes that make your spouse as happy as you are capable, even if you totally get your own way without making these changes.

Therefore, if you are capable, you have no excuse!

I realize that you have to heal. But you cannot begin to heal until you forgive, stop being a perpetual victim, and be accountable for your part in the marital discord.

Are you seriously presuming that your attitude or past withholding has absolutely nothing to do with your spouse's negative or unacceptable actions?

And do you truly believe that your self-focus and negative feelings towards your spouse will do anything to change your spouse, other than imposing guilt and other negative feelings?

Please don't try to fool yourself. You indeed know those areas of your marriage you are withholding and the excuses you are using to justify your actions. Regardless of your reasoning and rationalizations, the end result will be the same when you withhold – less than a 100% marriage.

Do you presume that giving less than 100% love in response to receiving 100% love will result in your spouse giving more love to you at some future point?

So stop using your children, job, financial status, the past, and yes, your spouse, as your excuses for giving less than you are capable.

Please also stop acting like you are living with an enemy, as opposed to a spouse. Yes, stop with the negative "comes backs" when your spouse brings something to your attention that is displeasing. As mentioned before, your response should be, *What is it that I need to do to make your negative feelings towards me disappear?* And I guarantee you that your posititve or negative attitude will be at the heart of your spouse's response.

Yes, in a sense, I am reprimanding you again.

But, in reality, I am trying once more to wake you up and deprogram you from the garbage you have learned and internalized from a culture that, to a large degree, has abandoned the notion of absolutes and redefined love to mean *get,* instead of *give.* Also, it upsets me to the maximum to know that you and millions of others are stuck on a marital treadmill without a compass and are going in the wrong direction. I want you and your spouse to be totally happy in your marriage. But it will require you to make the necessary changes for this to occur.

Remember, it doesn't take long.

Please also resist being a perpetual victim. You know, as well as I do, that victims don't have to change, nor do they have to accept responsibility for being part of the problem in a marriage. I realize that your spouse isn't perfect. My concern is that you may not be seeing your part in your marital problems. In the same way that the invisible wind behind the sail drives a boat, your real issues are most likely being re-enacted with your spouse. Rather than judging or psychoanalyzing your spouse and the possible reasons behind your marital problems, I am urging you to embrace love and what love really does.

If you want real answers to your marital problems, please keep reading.

By this point in your marriage, your spouse knows you quite well and can therefore easily determine your real attitude in meeting his or her needs. Your inconsistency in initiating the fulfillment of them speaks louder than words. Therefore, it may be premature for you to assert that you have tried everything and nothing works.

I must continue to stress that, as long as you continue to embrace your feelings of victimization and/or rate yourself as 100% as a spouse, figuratively speaking, you will stay stuck on *Route 95 North* and never achieve a mutually satisfying and completely harmonious marriage.

While you may insist that you are not selfish or crazy, settling for anything less than 100% simply does not make sense. Once again, would you settle for less than 100% fidelity in your marriage? Then why would you settle for anything less than getting and giving 100% in other areas of your marriage?

Are you obsessing and ruminating about the changes that you (not your spouse) need to make in your marriage, in the same way that you would obsess and ruminate about your spouse's past lover if infidelity had actually occurred in your marriage?

If your spouse had a lover, you would ask, *What did I do to deserve this?* or assert, *Regardless of my shortcomings, I didn't deserve to be cheated on!*

Am I right?

Why not ask yourself this question if your spouse appears to be unhappy or is emotionally distant or argumentative?

Ask yourself these questions:

- Is my spouse afraid to give me an honest answer?

- Does my spouse have to pause and contemplate a response to my question for fear of my reaction?

- Am I willing to want to know what would make my spouse 100% happy, 100% of the time?

People fear their enemies. Why does your spouse fear you?

Until your spouse feels completely safe in giving you an honest response, you cannot hope for a connecting and happy marriage.

If your spouse is feeling 90% safe, then he or she is struggling with 10% fear.

Would you settle for 90% fidelity?

Only you can create and maintain the safety that will result in your spouse trusting you enough to be completely honest.

Perhaps you spouse is attempting to protect you as a result of your outbursts or depressive reaction whenever honesty is *put under the light.*

Please don't get me wrong. You are just as entitled to getting your marital needs met completely too. However, the dynamic between you must change, and that dynamic can and will change in 15 seconds or less when you change the direction of your course.

Give What You Want to Get!

In the same way that you have learned that the simple flipping of a switch will turn a light on, you will similarly come to be convinced that, the simple act of putting love into actual practice will generate a love response.

It doesn't take long ... oh, about 15 seconds or less!

But you must do this in every area of your marriage and maintain your focus on what you need to be giving, as opposed to what you haven't been getting.

To convey an essential principle that underlies my 100% love approach, I often ask the husband in my counseling session what I would get if I punched him right in the face. The answer is always the same, *You would get a punch back in your face!*

Yes, indeed I would ... and I wouldn't even have to ask for one. All I would have to do is to give a punch to get a punch.

I will get what I have given, and the response is automatic – like turning on a light switch.

Thus, in short, <u>the principle here is simple</u>:

Give to your spouse what you want to get from your spouse!

Put Love Unconditionally into Action

Give what you want to get and the response you receive will be automatic.

Give love and in some form you will get love.

Never forget that love gives with the hope of getting in return, not with the condition or guarantee of getting in return. Giving with the right motive that is rooted in your heart is true, not artificial, love.

Thus, if you have been responding to your spouse's withholding, take the driver's seat by shifting your attitude and thinking in a way that conforms to love. Get back onto Route 95 South and stay there. You will get what you give.

Perhaps, in some form, without realizing it, you have been getting from your spouse what you have been giving.

If your spouse has been contentious, perhaps his or her behavior has been a reaction to your negative attitude and behavior.

Oh yes, I'm sure that you will insist that you are not perfect for sure, but you don't deserve how you have been treated.

If I have been accurate, in terms of what you are thinking at this moment, although I have never met you, perhaps I can convince you that after 33 years of professional experience and intense study I have discovered various universal principles about love and marriage that you can count on benefiting you.

Just as sure as everyone would turn around (in 15 seconds or less of course) if someone in the back of a church and began screaming obscenities at the top of their lungs, putting love into practice will generate a love response from your spouse.

I am not attempting to question your motive for maximizing your marriage; I am confronting your ineffective methods.

If, indeed, everything you have tried has not worked, your motives cannot be in question; your methods are. So, with hopeful anticipation, continue your reading with the mindset that your marital situation will begin to dramatically change quickly once you change your methods to conform to a *love response.*

Remember, the changes you are being asked to make are no more (or less) than what love requires. Therefore, if your attitude is right, once you make the needed changes, the solutions to all of your marital problems are but 15 seconds or less away!

Stay on course; Florida is closer than you think!

Chapter 3

Marital Portrait of Love

For a moment, let's briefly take a look at the face of love; that is, what love is, what it looks like, and what it does.

And let's not forget that you vowed to love your spouse for a lifetime, as you likewise vowed to be faithful to your spouse for a lifetime, each and every day for the rest of your married life.

Also, consider this – could there be any relationship between your spouse's indifference, distance, or negative attitude with your actions or withholding?

Well, what is your answer?

The good news is that you can get right back on track in your marriage by embracing the basics of your marital vows. Yes, your marital vows are essential and foundational to attaining your marriage miracle in response to every conceivable marital challenge.

So let's examine your marital vows for a moment. These vows represent the embodiment of your total commitment to your spouse that, in turn, can be fulfilled in one simple word – love.

And love can be put into action at any given point in time in 15 seconds or less!

Keep in mind that the word *love* is spelled G-I-V-E.

The Marital Vows and Their Meaning

Marital Vow	Meaning
To Have and To Hold	To possess or keep with your hands and arms; to have sex with.
To Love	To willingly give of oneself for your spouse's highest good. To Christians, the manner in which love is to be demonstrated should conform to 1 Corinthians 13: 4-7.
To Honor	To treat one's spouse with high regard and great respect, in a manner fitting to a King or Queen.
To Cherish	To hold dear and take excellent care of.
To Comfort	To sooth in distress or sorrow, and be an encourager.
To be Faithful	To exhibit fidelity, devotion and loyalty; to not forsake for another.
For Better or For Worse	For better or for worse!
For Richer or For Poorer	To be satisfied and content with the material possessions that are provided by your spouse.
In Sickness and In Health	To stay married and devoted, regardless of the physical or emotional state of one's spouse.
Till Death Do Us Part	To remain married for a lifetime, till your imperfect spouse passes away.

The Face and Behavior of Love

At the beginning of most Christian ceremonies, the couple typically chooses a reading from 1 Corinthians, Chapter 13, the *love* chapter. I'm sure that you can practically recall most, if not all, of the verses that are read from this chapter that exemplify the actual qualities of love:

Patient (or long-suffering)

Kind

Not boastful

Not jealous

Not arrogant

Does not act unbecomingly

Does not seek its' own

Does not take into account wrongs suffered

Does not rejoice in unrighteousness

Rejoices with the truth

Bears all things

Believes all things

Hopes all things

Endures all things

Never fails.

In consideration of your vow to love and, in consideration of what love demands, please answer the following questions to yourself:

- Have you been consistently "faithful" to your marital vows, in terms of exhibiting the attitudes that underlie putting love into practice?

Each and every day during your marriage:

- Have you been 100% patient … or have you ever been reactive?
- Have you been 100% kind … or have you ever been unkind?

25

- Have you been 100% not boastful ... or have you ever criticized your spouse or unfavorably compared your spouse's shortcomings to yourself or others?

- Have you not been jealous 100% of the time ... or have you ever unfairly accused your spouse of desiring someone else or being more fond of someone else than you?

- Have you been refrained from not being arrogant towards your spouse 100% of the time ... or have you ever been overbearing towards your spouse and over-focused on your needs, as opposed to your spouses'.

- Have you never acted unbecomingly 100% of the time towards your spouse ... or have you ever acted in an offensive or inappropriate way towards your spouse?

- Have you, 100% of the time, never sought your own interests or way in your marriage ... or have you ever gotten your own way at the expense of what would make your spouse's happy?

- Have you, 100% of the time, never taken into accounts wrongs suffered by your spouse ... or have you ever criticized your spouse or brought up matters regarding your spouse's past behaviors that hurt or offended you?

The last three words, *Love never fails*, of what is cited from the love chapter during the typical wedding ceremony, absolutely embraces the main message of this book.

Marriages succeed when love is practiced and indeed fall short or fail when it is not!

Now, have you been "unfaithful," in terms of keeping all of your marriage vows?

Are you willing to admit that you have broken the, *to love* vow?

And, at various time, the other marital vows, as well?

Could you be getting what you have been giving?

If you have broken any of your marital vows, how do you reason that you are in a position of calling the shots, with respect to selectively determining which marital needs you will or will not meet?

Unfortunately, in our society today, marriage has been redefined or mischaracterized in so many different ways that, figuratively speaking, many who are attempting to get to Florida are finding themselves somewhere stuck in a snow bank in the Arctic!

How close are you to arriving to Florida from where you are in your marriage?

At this point, perhaps you may be thinking, in so many words, *Oh, I now get it; the author of this book has a radical, right-winged philosophy!*

If you are thinking this: *No, I am a right-armed author who knows that putting love into practice is right. I have no "wings," as well. But, since you contemplated the issue of wings, that is, my philosophy, I do recall how the quality of love was long-ago depicted by a most prudent and insightful woman, named Hannah Whitall Smith.*

According to Hannah:

> *Love gives all, and must have all in return. The wishes of one become the binding obligations to the other, and the deepest desire of each heart is that it may know every secret wish or longing of the other, in order that it may fly on the wings of the wind to gratify it.* [3]

Now isn't this the type of marriage you would like to have?

Why would you even contemplate settling for anything less?

Believe it or not, my wife, Mary, made Hannah's depiction of the nature of love recently come alive in my marriage. And I feel absolutely compelled to write about it.

My wife and I are cyclists. For Christmas I informed her that the present that would make me the happiest is if I could purchase a new bicycle. Unfortunately, the sales price of the bicycle is approximately $1800.00. Given our current financial status, this purchase is far out of our financial reach.

Nevertheless, without my asking, my wife grabbed her diamond engagement ring and said that she was willing to sell it so the purchase of the bike would be possible.

My wife had tears in her eyes, depicting her degree of sincerity.

While under no condition would I ever agree to her selling her engagement ring, needless to say, I was very touched and continue to contemplate her loving gesture every day.

In fact, this one loving act drives me to reciprocate in many small ways throughout the day, with the hope that I can reciprocate in a very big way sometime in the future.

And she has no idea that her willingness to do such a thing was the biggest and best Christmas present I could ever ask for! Yet one thing is for certain, I will not be at rest till I find the thing that makes her the happiest and bless her heart with it!

This is but one example of how love works and its' impact in a marriage.

Financially, my wife and I struggle each month to pay our bills. But what we have is something that is worth more than all of the money in the world, yet it's free. It's free for you too. Why pass up any chance to love your spouse by meeting his or her most pressing needs?

Give No Less Than 100%

You've said your marital vows at the marriage alter, so do your part in keeping them. Remember, you are going to get what you give. Also, keep in mind that *two becoming one* means that your independence is limited. In this regard, you are accountable to your spouse and his or her happiness as well, each and every day, 100% of the time.

Also, please consider the fact that you and your spouse became one entity by the marital covenant that was exchanged between you. Consequently, the two of you became a part of the whole. Thus, if you give 50% and your spouse gives 50% and then you multiply it, you will end up with 25%. The more each of you give, the higher the marital rating. The spouse that gives the most will bring the marriage to a higher level and have a positive impact on the spouse who gives the least.

At this point, do you believe that 100% giving is unreasonable?

It is not unreasonable to expect fidelity 100% of the time, each and every day, right?

Then what gives you the right to give less and also expect less than the 100% fulfillment of all of your marital vows, each and every day as long as you both shall live?

In short, both you and your spouse are entitled to get all of your marital needs met to the fullest of each others' satisfaction. Aside from a physical disability or true emergency, there is no good excuse for withholding if you are capable.

You expect your spouse to remain faithful whether he or she feels like it or not, right?

If I should challenge you regarding your belief that you are entitled to fidelity, would you not justify your answer on the sole basis that you and your spouse said marital vows and, thus, this entitles you to fidelity 100% of the time?

Then how can you or anyone else stake claim to the notion that the other remaining marital vows are not subject to the *100% of the time* requirement?

Spouses who want all of their marital needs met are often called *control freaks*. Should we call you a *control freak* for expecting fidelity all day long, each and every day, and for the rest of your married life? Should we also assert that you have a *one-track mind*?

With due respect, if you are now saying, *Oh, that's different!* you are definitely wrong. Why? There is no basis whatsoever for withholding other than pure selfishness. Selfishness, the withholding of a marital need onto "one-self," is not love in practice but, rather, an end result of fear. As already indicated several times, fear is what controls your thinking and, henceforth, your dispositions and actions. It is something that you have learned and it is something that is continuously being reinforced in this mixed up society that sees nothing but shades of gray in everything! Therefore, most couples are headed toward Maine in northern United States, believing they are on route to Disney World on the southern side.

If you embrace shades of gray in various aspects of your marriage, such as the issue of meeting all of your spouse's marital needs, then don't complain why your spouse sees shades of gray where it comes meeting your most important needs, including fidelity. If you choose *cafeteria-style thinking* wherein the practice of love becomes reduced to, *I'll embrace a little of this aspect of love, if and when I feel like it*, or *...when I get my needs met first*, you'll end up with a second-rate *cafeteria-style* marriage.

Prepare a gourmet banquet for your spouse in every area of your marriage. Why? Because what you prepare is what you will be able to sit down and enjoy!

Also, stop playing word games to get out of meeting a marital need. In this regard, you may assert, *It's not a need; it's a want!* This is analogous to me asserting that infidelity won't kill you if you don't get it, so this is a "want."

I bet you just flinched after reading that comment.

Simply stated, a *marital need* is a desire that, when fulfilled, will result in your spouse's happiness.

Individuals who simply wish to continue being selfish or in promoting it, immediately look for far-fetched examples of how the meeting of marital needs can be unreasonable or extreme. Bringing a third party into your marital bedroom is not an example of a marital need because it violates the letter of the marital vow, *To be faithful*. However, withholding legitimate marital needs violates the, *To love*, marital vow. I consider not keeping the, *To love*, vow to be as far-fetched as you can get!

We are created to love and, when we get married, we vow to love ... to death do us part. Therefore, not putting love into practice is a perversion at its' very core. It is!

In general, why would you resist wanting to meet any of your spouse's marital needs? Perhaps your spouse has had to suffer more by having to tolerate the painful deprivation of his or her marital needs being met for years that other spouses routinely meet. Does that bother you that they do and you don't? If your heart is right, it should. If you are committed to putting love into action, you will.

If, in fact, it does, who should then be doing the changing, you or your spouse? For once in your life, take charge of and, consequently, be free of fear! Once again, the evidence of fear is defensiveness that takes the form or withholding and, thus, breaking a marital vow.

How can you say that you are keeping the, *To Honor* vow, while being reactive, argumentative, or simply ignoring what you know in your heart will make your spouse happy?

Why wait 15 seconds? Forsake fear this very moment by not being selfish!

Make the change and be free! You will also be free from an unhappy marriage.

If you don't want to be controlled, then take control of fear. And don't confuse being controlled with fulfilling the obligations that you committed to when you exchanged your marital vows. Your spouse made them as well. Marriage comes with rights and responsibilities, not one or the other.

And resist all other notions of cafeteria-style pick-n-choose-type giving. Your spouse is entitled to more than that!

Also, stop attempting to *barter* with your spouse!

You are probably thinking, *I don't know what you mean?*

You know exactly what I mean. Stop putting conditions on your giving. Change the mindset that says, *I'll do such and such for you if or when you do such and such for me.*

How would you like it if someone bought you a birthday present and then expected you to pay for it? You would conclude that you were not truly given anything and, consequently, would return it to the giver. So, how do you think it feels when you give only if your spouse gives you what you want in advance? Please answer the question before you read on.

Just as it is incredulously audacious to expect payment for giving a present, it is likewise audacious to expect the same where marital needs are involved.

This is the point where you are going to insist that you have given and given and given, have done so throughout your marriage, have nothing else left to give, and would be sending your spouse the message that he or she can continue to walk all over you unless you take drastic action.

Are you willing to hear the truth from your spouse about all of the things you have said and done that have either hurt or shortchanged him or her?

Could it be that you have withheld one or two marital needs that carry the greatest amount of weight, with respect to making your spouse happy or fulfilled?

There is nothing wrong with hoping that your spouse will reciprocate. But mandating reciprocation is indeed an act of bartering. Remember, love gives unconditionally with the hope, not requirement, of getting in return. The true meaning behind the receiving is what the giving represents. For sure, it represents being loved.

Please consider what you know would make your spouse the happiest.

Are you meeting this marital need?

And are you meeting this need consistently and to the fullest extent possible to keep your spouse consistently happy?

If you are not, you are sending your spouse the message, *I don't love you.*

And if you are sending your spouse this message, you are breaking your marriage vow, *to love.*

I am sure that you have rarely or never heard about love in the manner in which it is being framed. That is why I am truly excited that you are reading this book. I find myself not being able to wait longer than 15 seconds to hear about how your marriage has been transformed and how happy you and your spouse now are!

Also, the weight of the marital need must be considered as well.

The greater the weight of your spouse's marital need, the more loved your spouse will feel if this marital need is met. This is why infidelity hurts so much; the marital need of faithfulness carries a great weight.

Have you made it your business to determine, not only what your spouse's most important marital needs are but, also, the weight of them?

What unmet marital need does your spouse always seem to complain about?

What unmet marital need does your spouse appear to be obsessed about?

Even if your spouse does not complain, what does your gut tell you about the marital need(s) that you are not meeting at all or to your spouse's satisfaction?

Are you willing to accept responsibility on your part for loving your spouse 100%?

If you do not care enough to find out about what would make your spouse the happiest, you are certainly embracing a double standard, while shortchanging your spouse and thus breaking your marital vow of *to love*.

But it's not too late to change … and it only takes 15 seconds or less!

The Negative Impact of Shortchanging Your Spouse

Please consider if you would trust your spouse if he or she was only faithful 90% of the time? How about 99% of the time?

Wouldn't you agree that your spouse could not boast about being faithful unless fidelity was being practiced 100% of the time?

Then how can you boast about being faithful in keeping your other marriage vows unless you have kept them 100% of the time?

As an illustration, regarding the issue of the impact of shortchanging your spouse, suppose I were to ask you to give me a dollar in exchange for change that I had in my pocket. Would you trust me anymore if I only chose to give you 90 cents in return, even though I had more than a dollar of change in my pocket?

I predict that you would not trust me anymore and certainly not count me as a friend as well. And it would really hurt you because we were close before you were shortchanged by me to something that you were entitled.

If someone then challenged you about the issue of writing off our friendship over a mere ten cents, you would say, *It's not the money; it's the principle!*

And wouldn't you admit that our relationship would never be the same after this "less than 15 seconds" transaction?

This is what occurs in marriages when one spouse shortchanges the other to any degree in completely fulfilling the letter and spirit of any of the marriage vows.

Now that you can see how shortchanging your spouse negatively impacts your marriage, you are in a great position to begin making immediate changes. In fact, you can decide to make these changes in, oh ... about 15 seconds or less!

Perhaps your excuse for not meeting one or more of your spouse's marital needs is that he (or she) will survive. Yes, not meeting a marital need will not kill anyone, but it sure will certainly kill the trust and feelings of regard from the spouse being shortchanged. Therefore, you must admit that if you have shortchanged your spouse, you are indeed part of the problem.

Also, do not fool yourself into believing that you have married a high-maintenance person and therefore could be better matched with someone else. If everyone thought this way, we would all probably be re-married about two dozen times at a minimum.

Marital needs are universal. Therefore, you are likely to be in for a big surprise if you bring this type of thinking to a different mate and expect a different result.

While preferences may vary, the time to choose Mr. or Mrs. Right or Mr. or Mrs. Soul-Mate is before, not after, you have made a lifetime commitment to your spouse and to God, *for better or for worse, till death do you part.*

Ask the greatest victims of divorce, your children, what they think.

Are you coming up with *Yes, but ...* or *How about if ...* questions again after reading this? Until this type of thinking changes, you are going to be broken down on a road leading to nowhere but unhappiness. As your thinking changes, your behaviors will follow, accordingly.

If you have already re-married and are considering divorce (i.e., a way out from the effects of love not being practiced), please try embracing and applying what love requires and you may indeed have second thoughts ... in 15 seconds or less!

The Characteristics of Real Commitment

Keeping your marital vows also requires commitment. Commitment has nothing to do whatsoever with being motivated to keep your vows. In actuality, it involves being faithful to your marital vows.

Would you like it if your spouse was faithful only if and when you met all of his or her marital needs? Then likewise consider how your spouse feels when you are not faithful in meeting another need that is very important to him or her. Hopefully, you will make the change(s) that are needed to put 100% love into practice in your marriage.

With that being said, let's take a look at what a truly committed spouse says and does.

The characteristics of real commitment are as follows:

1. Not having to be told to follow-through.

2. Not experiencing resentment or annoyance to meeting your spouse's marital needs.

3. The commonly stated excuses, *I forgot*; *I didn't really know*; *Something came up*; *I was busy with the kids*; or props, such as, *Would you remind me?* are not used or needed by you, the giver.

4. You consider your sacred marriage vows when in the midst of a marital crisis.

5. Temptation confronts you straight-on, but you successfully resist giving into it.

6. You accept 100% responsibility for your actions and reactions.

7. You make the necessary changes to fulfill the letter and spirit of your marriage vows, regardless of your spouse's behavior or attitude.

Please be honest; have you been totally and completely committed to your marriage? If you haven't, why not make a decision to be so in 15 seconds or less?

Avoid Shortchanging Your Marriage by Negotiating Marital Needs

There is absolutely no room for *negotiating* or compromising with respect to meeting all of your spouse's marital needs. Therefore, if you are asked to consider negotiating with your spouse to arrive at a mid-point by anyone, including a mental health professional or Pastor, you are simply receiving bad advice; you are being directed to embrace the notion of being a "50% spouse" which culminates in a "25% marriage."

Please consider the process of negotiating to purchase a car. Isn't it true that your goal is to give as little as possible in order to get as much as possible? I rest my case.

Love gives 100% with the goal of meeting the other's needs 100%. If 100% is the standard for love, how could you consider negotiating a marital need? For example, if your spouse wishes to negotiate fidelity, would you be willing?

Suppose he or she would like to be faithful to you 5 days a week, whereas you would like faithfulness to occur 7 days a week.

Would you be willing be negotiate? Would you be willing to compromise? Would you be willing to "meet in the middle"?

If you would surely expect your white laundry to be contaminated by darks that were thrown in the washer and dryer together, why would you likewise think that withholding would not contribute to a non-loving response from your spouse? And that includes every aspect of marriage, including sex. It also includes meeting the remainder of your spouse's needs when you are very upset with him or her.

In actuality, acts of withholding or selfishness contaminate the flow of pure love in a marriage. However, in the same way that whitener will indeed remove the color from the whites, acts of love through the practice of meeting 100% of your spouse's marital needs will likewise remove the negative effects upon the marriage by past acts of selfishness.

Separating the darks from the whites takes about 15 seconds or less. Starting the process of putting your love into action should take less time than that.

Incidentally, did you say your marriage vows to your children, or boss, or friends or anyone or, in fact, to anything else? Therefore, take no pride if you have been putting these individuals or things before your spouse. Just like you did not sign-up for second place when you were exchanging your vows, neither did your spouse. Therefore, begin putting your spouse in his or her rightful place of #1. Your children won't die if you do, but your marriage may die if you don't!

Please don't develop a, *How dare you!* or *I don't care what you think!* attitude regarding my advice regarding my recommendation that your spouse's needs should be held in first priority over your children. Making them over-dependent on you does the opposite of what you intend; it weakens them and contributes to them developing narcissistic and oppositional dispositions, many of which are mischaracterized as ADHD symptomatology.

Paradoxically, an unfulfilled and needy spouse tends to lack initiative and can often be seen sitting around the house, spaced-out or over-reactive to the smallest shortcomings or slights to family members.

How would you characterize the emotional climate of your home?

Once you begin putting your spouse first and in focusing on meeting his or her martial needs to the fullest possible extent, the attainment of your marital oneness and, "a house <u>not</u> divided" will undeniably benefit the children and enable you and your spouse to work together as an effective marital team in the challenge of co-parenting to your children's highest benefit.

At this point, as you are learning more about marital love, is the notion of 15 seconds or less sound more reasonable?

Also, compare what is being presented in this book to what you have read, been taught, or advised.

Have you been misled?

The media has often contributed to distortions regarding what constitutes a happy and healthy marriage. For example, a husband's need for a non-contentious, non-controlling, committed and dutiful wife has been mocked and distorted in the film, *The Stepford Wives*.

While I would agree that all husbands would cherish the types of behaviors that the *Stepford* wives exhibited in this movie, the implicit lies promoted in it are that husbands want mindless wives, that husbands by nature do not have a disposition of reciprocating love, and meeting all of one's husband's marital needs as an act of marital devotion is tantamount to being a slave and mindless wife in a second-rate, one-sided marriage.

Hopefully, you feel a pull within you develop coupled with a spark of optimism as you learn about the transforming miracle power of love, and are deprogrammed from the post-modern propaganda that likens sacrificial giving to being taken for granted and abused.

Helping you to realize all of your marital dreams is my goal for writing this book. My style of straight-talk to you is not any attempt on my part to be offensive but, rather, my attempt to get you unstuck and on route to attaining your marriage miracle.

You have been stuck for years.

Why?

This simple answer is because most people who write about the topic of marital love and marital responsibilities are "in the dark," so to speak. The rest are afraid of offending you. Yes, other's fear has been to your detriment. This has reinforced your posture and disposition of being a victim and then becoming defensive when the truth is brought to your attention. Unfortunately, this gets transmitted and conveyed to your children.

You are closer than you think in receiving your marriage miracle. Keep on reading, as the remainder of this book highlights practical steps you can take to reaching your intended destination, *the perfect marriage*.

While I don't claim to be the only person on the planet who knows what they are talking about on this topic, I hope that this book enlightens many to change their views and put their audience and readers on the right track. Keep on reading, as I outline the framework and specifics for maximizing your spouse's response.

In what time frame? You guessed it!

Chapter 4

Quality Time: Key to a Mutually-Fulfilling Marriage

Obtaining an adequate amount of marital quality time is absolutely essential to achieving a healthy and mutually-fulfilling marriage that is exciting, interesting, and ever-growing. In short, marital quality time produces a quality marriage. It cements and sustains the marital relationship. This is most evident in newly married couples taking a honeymoon and in couples celebrating their wedding anniversary.

In consideration of the illustration that I have used wherein arriving in Florida from a northern location represents mutual marital satisfaction and fulfillment, obtaining adequate marital quality time is the vehicle used to arrive to Florida.

The fuel in this vehicle is heart and commitment.

What type of fuel is in your heart?

Nevertheless, in my counseling with couples, this is where I typically get a lot of resistance from both spouses, typically in 15 seconds or less.

Minimum Amount of Marital Quality Time for a Quality Marriage

My firm recommendation is that <u>every couple must get a minimum of 15 hours of marital quality time together per week</u>. This is, in fact, one recommendation that most, if not all, couples would have preferred me saying those magical words, *15 seconds or less.*

After exhibiting a demeanor that can best be described as one that would be seen by a deer looking at a car's headlights, in so many words I am told, *We can't do that!* This is followed by the question, *So what do you mean by marital quality time?*

What is Marital Quality Time?

Marital quality time is time spent together that you and your spouse enjoy at the same time.

Marital quality time can fall into any one of the following 3 general categories:

1. Intimacy

2. Fun

3. Companionship.

Intimacy involves:

- words and acts of affection
- deep and heartfelt discussions
- being romantic
- sexual intimacy
- communicating in an endearing way etc.

Fun involves:

- watching television shows that are of mutual interest
- being playful
- developing and practicing common interests
- going on a vacation
- going out on a date with each other

- engaging in a mutually-enjoyable hobby together
- developing an interest in a hobby or interest that your spouse enjoys etc.

Companionship involves:

- being there for your mate when he or she needs you,
- working together as a team to fulfill household responsibilities,
- discussing time schedules, chores, bills, repair work, and problems,
- working out win-win solutions to issues affecting the relationship,
- shopping together, engaging in growth-related activities, listening etc.

Companionship creates a strong bond resulting from spouses sharing and enjoying each other's company as one would with a special friend.

In terms of meeting your spouse's need for marital quality time, the weight of your spouse's marital need certainly comes into play in conjunction with your commitment to meet it.

For example, if your spouse's greatest quality time marital need is affection and you are not providing it or are providing it only what is asked, you can only hope for a quality marriage by sheer luck.

Consequently, your spouse's perception of the marriage as being a quality marriage will only occur in infrequent small spurts.

I am certain that this is not the kind of marriage that you desire or have dreamed of.

The importance of developing similar interests has been gaining increasing attention among the helping professions. In this regard, the research consistently supports the importance and power of similar interests in a marriage.

These findings strongly suggest that there is a correlation between the quantity of time spouses spend with each other and marital satisfaction. Therefore, developing and/or practicing common interests are essential to the marriage.

In the next section on the following page, I have constructed a list of various quality time activities for you and your spouse to contemplate for enriching your marriage.

In addition, 3 questions are provided as a means of facilitating follow-through on your part.

Various Quality Time Activities to Consider With Your Spouse

Listed below are a number of quality time activities to consider with your spouse.

Going out to dinner | Going to the movies | Sightseeing | Bird feeding | Gardening | Power-boating | Rock climbing | Scuba diving | Walking | Going to amusement parks | Archery | Camping | Going to a zoo | Bowling | Barbecuing | Visiting a museum | Going to the city | Watching t.v. | Picnicking | Going to the sea shore | Cycling | Sailing | Fishing | Swimming | Home repair | Ice skating | Skiing | Going to a flea market | Video-game playing | Baking | Painting | Visiting a museum | Stargazing | Playing ice hockey | Playing ping pong | Playing pool | Visiting a light house | Visiting a farm market | Decorating | Kite flying | Playing miniature golf | Golfing | Playing computer games | Playing a board game | Card-playing | Planning a social event | Visiting a relative or friend | Praying together | Joining a co-ed sport | Going to church together | Wine tasting | Listening to music | Learning a musical instrument | Drawing | Ballroom dancing | Taking a course together | Backpacking | Taking a martial art | Canoeing | Touring | Playing darts | Going to a club | Dancing | Playing frisbee | Going to the mall | Jogging | Mountain biking | Playing tennis | Traveling | Going to a fitness center | Snowmobiling | Boating | Learning a new skill | Taking a college course | Shopping | Taking a history tour | Taking a seminar | Creative cooking | Going to a play | Taking an overnight getaway | Going to the beach |

Instructions to Spouses:

1. Pick your top 5 quality time activities from the list above and share them with your spouse.

2. Make the time to engage in some of these quality time activities with your spouse within the next 2 weeks.

3. Make a list of activities that you would like to do that you have not done together as a couple, and then make plans to do them in the near future.

Vacationing

It is very important for married couples to take at least a one-week vacation and two weekend vacations together per year. These need to be taken without the children.

Are you ready to *put your money where your mouth is* and start worrying more about the need for private marital quality time with your spouse, as opposed to your children's secondary needs?

There are a number of ways to vacation without spending "an arm and a leg" if you will take the time to research the Internet and ask questions to friends regarding how to go on an affordable vacation.

Many couples are members of travel or vacations clubs and also have timeshares. Some timeshares and vacations clubs provide access to excess inventory or getaways that you could legitimately make use of through the membership of a number of your friends and relatives.

My wife and I have a vacation club membership that, in fact, provides us a weekly list of excess inventory. Last year, we selected an available condo on two occasions, within a few miles from *Downtown Disney*, to make maximum use of our *Disney World Annual Passholder Membership* of which cost my wife and I collectively a total of $999.00 at that time. It only cost us $188.00 per week each time we selected the available condo from the *Excess Inventory* list. We have also saved money by riding our car to Florida, as opposed to taking a plane and then having to rent a car for transportation. It costs us approximately $250.00 for gasoline and tolls per trip to *Disney World* from New Jersey.

Incidentally, we take *Interstate 95 South* to get to Florida!

To save additional money on our *Disney World* vacation, we stock our condo with food and eat at inexpensive restaurants outside the parks. Do the math, not including food, it cost my wife and I approximately $487.50 for our last 2 *Disney World* vacations.

There is a number of relatively affordable *All-Inclusive*-type of packages deals for vacationers throughout the world. All you simply have to do is to use your Internet search engine, speak with a travel agent, contact AAA, or simply ask a friend.

Camping is also a very inexpensive way of having a romantic or family vacation from the Spring Season to the Fall.

Please resist making the excuse that you cannot afford to comply with my vacationing recommendations. Better said, you cannot afford not to comply with them. And an additional payoff of having a great time with your spouse will be in cultivating an exciting and mutually-fulfilling marriage with a very happy spouse.

Learn Your Spouse's Love Language

Author Gary Chapman has actually written an entire book on a couple's love languages, based upon his extensive interaction with married couples and personal research on what facilitates marital intimacy and connectedness. In his research, Dr. Chapman found that individuals feel love and are drawn to their spouses when each speaks love in the language of the other. In addition to words of affirmation, physical touch, gifts, and acts of service, he cites quality time as one of the dominant *5 love languages* of married couples. [4]

When a spouse, such as my wife, cites marital *quality time* as the highest love language, it is absolutely crucial that the weight and impact of this need not be underestimated. Why? Because you will never be completely happy in your marriage, unless this marital need is met to your satisfaction.

Has your spouse confirmed that you completely and, yes, consistently met all of his or her needs for marital quality time?

Prioritize Making Marital Quality Time

Getting adequate marital quality time should not be used as filler space in a gap of time that is convenient in the midst of childrearing, housekeeping, work and other types of necessary responsibilities. It should be prioritized and be a way of life! If it is not, you will never have anything more than a mediocre marriage.

My wife and I have had 5 children and have consistently gotten a minimum of 15 hours of marital quality time a week throughout our marriage. Therefore, so can you!

At this point, are you equating marital quality time as a chore or as a much needed answer to your marital problems?

Does the thought of being recommended to get a minimum of 15 hours out of a 168 hour week feel overwhelming to you?

Are you feeling annoyed like many couples who want a major overhaul in their marriage, yet insist on keeping their focus on everything but their marriage?

You may be asking yourself, *how am I going to find the time with my current schedule and all of my responsibilities?* Please consider the fact that you must first make the time for marital quality time before you can find the time.

In short, **you will never find the time unless you first make the time.**

Secondly, prioritizing everything but your marriage will have predictable results – a second rate marriage!

This is not what you signed up for when you said, *I do.* So begin putting your marriage in first position. It shouldn't take you more than 15 seconds to decide.

Incidentally, once again, did you say marital vows to your children, your boss, your creditors, or your friends? Then why have you been putting them first? Why is your energy tank on *Empty* at the end of the day when your spouse needs you the most?

Admit it – you have deliberately failed to prioritize your marriage. And don't use the excuse that your spouse hasn't shown any interest either, that your spouse is too *high-maintenance*, or that your children need you. These justifications are what got your marriage to where it is – a co-existent one. In co-existent marriages, spouses simply do little more than live together in a boring and non-connecting marriage according to a rather set routine.

Continuing to use these justifications will keep you stuck, not on the way to Florida but, rather in an emotional snow bank somewhere up in the northern part of the world.

Get back on Route 95 South or from your current location the direction that leads you to Florida, and then put your foot on the gas. The more time you spend getting marital quality time, the faster you will arrive in Florida.

If you ignore this bit of advice everyone, including your children, will suffer!

Instead of spoiling your children any longer, devote the majority of your time, attention, and energy on your spouse.

Accept responsibility for your actions, rather than blaming everything and everyone else. Moreover, contemplate what have you said or done to make yourself interesting and exciting to your spouse If your life depended on it, what would you do differently to get your poor or coexistent marriage back on track? Whatever it is, begin doing it now!

Please keep in mind that you and your spouse must be mutually and simultaneously experience time together as quality time together, as opposed to simply spending time together. Otherwise, your marital time spent together does not count as marital quality time.

Attempt to develop at least one common ongoing interest together. For example, my wife and I have joined a fitness center and go there together three times a week. We make the time after I get home from work at 9:00 PM. We train together to get in shape for our mutual goal of riding 100 miles on our bicycles and enjoying cycling as a lifestyle.

It is crucial that you get involved in your spouse's primary interest to facilitate marital oneness and closeness. For example, if your spouse loves golf, you should do all you can to learn everything about golf and to play it with your spouse as well.

Do you care enough to do this?

You certainly spend your fair share of time breaking up your children's fights, cleaning messes around the house, doing everything that is necessary to please your boss, and so forth.

Consider what it conveys to your spouse when you show little or no interest in the hobbies and pastimes that please him or her. Also, consider what little there actually is to talk about with your spouse from your current lifestyle and routine, aside from discussing the irritations of the day and what happened during the day. What happened talk gets boring real quick. So create a fulfilling marital life, by making the time for marital quality time. Do it now.

How to Be Your Spouse's Best Friend

Quite often, spouses express the desire to grow in their marriage to a point wherein they are each other's best friends. I consider this a very worthwhile marital goal. Yet, very few actually ever truly attempt to achieve this worthwhile goal.

For a moment, please consider how best friends actually treat each other. They accept each other unconditionally, accept each other's personal shortcomings, can communicate with each other without fear of criticism, share each other's interests, make sacrifices to maintain the friendship, fill in the gap during periods of loneliness, and are there for each other, even when their energy level is on "empty."

If you want your spouse to be your friend, be a friend!

Do you want a connecting marriage?

If you do, start connecting with your spouse.

How?

As a start, after making marital quality time, please stop talking about the following 5 topics of discussion:

1. The children

2. Work

3. Finances

4. Health

5. Things others have said or done that annoyed or upset you

Admit it. Aren't these the topics that you and your spouse repeatedly discuss around the house and even when you go out to dinner?

Wouldn't you agree with me that these topics do virtually nothing to promote romance, intimacy, or connectedness?

Please, at a minimum, greatly limit your discussion of these topics with your spouse.

Can you? Are you willing? Please get off of the marital treadmill you are on.

If you don't, you will stay on "stuck" in your marriage, and destined to go nowhere.

In response to this recommendation, one of my clients resentfully asked, *Then what are we going to talk about?*

My brief answer was: *How you feel about each other; a discussion about your next date or your future vacation; a discussion of your interests; a discussion of what makes you happy; relationship goals; what you are enjoying in the present; what new interests and hobbies you have been considering; your fantasies; what you would like to be doing more of; how much you love each other; your lifetime goals and a number of other things that you rarely or never discuss with each other!*

Questions to Consider to Turn the Key
to a Mutually-Fulfilling Marriage

Are you ready to engage with your spouse regarding his or her greatest interest?

Are you willing to inquire about your spouse's greatest marital quality time need?

Are you willing to learn about and speak in your spouse's love language?

Are you willing to make the changes that are necessary to be an exciting spouse?

Are you willing to make the time and spend the money for taking vacations with your spouse throughout the year?

Will you make those changes that are necessary to be perceived by your spouse as a best friend?

Will you commit to a minimum of 15 hours of marital quality time a week with your spouse?

Answering these questions in the affirmative is the key to attaining a mutually-fulfilling marriage.

Answering, *Yes,* to each of these questions should only take you 15 seconds or less.

If you have answered, *Yes,* you have just put your marriage in *drive.*

Chapter 5

Achieving Connecting Marital Communication

Communication can either be a bridge or stumbling block in a marriage.

Interestingly, by far, the vast majority of my incoming clients seeking couple's counseling assert that poor communication or a lack of communication is their major presenting problem. Do you believe that most, if not all, of your relational problems is the result of poor communication in your marriage?

Poor Communication: Strictly a Symptom of Marital Problems

As repeatedly stated, it is my view that communication difficulties in your relationship do not actually represent the primary problem but, rather, are symptoms of them. For example, when I ask my couples if they would be experiencing communication problems if they were getting all of their marital needs met their answer is always the same - "No."

Therefore, my point is simple – unmet marital needs is your problem.

If you are not meeting all of your spouse's marital needs and he or she is upset about it, you are part of the problem. This problem will not disappear if you simply learn how to communicate better; it will begin to disappear as you begin to meet those marital needs that are causing your spouse to be upset.

Do you find this proposition to be upsetting?

At this point, do you see that your spouse's actions towards you and reactions from you (whether they be passive or aggressive) are part of the dynamic that you both have created?

Learning effective communication skills will help you and your spouse to *manage* your relational problems for a short time but, alone, they will never be a suitable substitute for getting those unmet needs completely met.

Where to Focus Your Communication

Rather than getting off track by over-focusing on the tone of your spouse's voice or nonverbal mannerisms, please listen carefully to the content of what is being said. Focus on those unmet needs that are being brought to your attention.

Are you interested enough to find out what they are or would you prefer to stay stuck in terms of perceiving yourself as a victim?

Think about the last time your spouse appeared to be truly happy and content around you. What was different, in terms of how you were acting compared to how you are behaving now?

If you once made your spouse very happy, you have the ability to do so again. And based upon your enlightenment about love, you have a much greater ability to make your spouse happier. But first, you must come to the point of seeing that your spouse will find it nearly impossible to change to your liking while you are blaming, criticizing, bringing up the past, and withholding love while simultaneously wanting validation for these types of behaviors.

Can't you see that it doesn't make sense to expect a negative reaction from your spouse, in response to your indifference, antagonism, or self-centered focus?

For a moment, please put yourself in your spouse's position. How would you be responding if your spouse was acting exactly like you?

Are you feeling defensive right now – in 15 seconds or less after you have read the beginning of this paragraph?

If you are, please remember that it is your fear of accountability and change that is at the heart of your negative emotional reaction – not what you are reading and certainly not your spouse.

Oh, but you don't know what I've been through, Dr. Racite!
Yes, I do!

The "Police Effect"

A characteristic present in a situation where marital needs are not being met fully is where a spouse is afraid to bring these needs to the attention of his or her spouse.

Sound familiar?

There are moments in the marital relationship when spouses feel that they cannot verbalize disappointment, nor do they feel they can repeat themselves regarding an unmet marital need or, at times, verbalize a request.

I call this dynamic the *Police Effect*.

I am sure that there have been times in your life that you discover that you are being followed by a police car. When this happens, do you notice that you begin watching every move you make and, although you are staying on course, your experience as a driver is not the same? Anxiety is created which makes you feel uneasy and immobilized to a certain degree.

Now consider how you feel when you desire to bring a marital need to the attention of your spouse.

If you, to any degree, feel as you do when a police car is riding behind you, then you are experiencing the *Police Effect*.

To test whether this effect is present in your marital relationship, simply think about all of your marital needs and bring them to your spouse's attention.

- Do you desire more quality time from your spouse?

- Do you have a great need for your spouse to go to religious services with you on a regular basis?

- Do you need more affection?

- Do you need more connecting communication?

- Do you need money in order to buy a necessity?

- Are you completely satisfied with lovemaking with your spouse?

If all is well in your marriage, you should not experience any anxiety in making requests that would result in your marital needs being met fully. Neither should your spouse make you feel guilty or unreasonable regarding these needs.

Unfortunately, most married couples live, to some degree, in an alienated state in order to avoid getting a ticket, so to speak. Do you act like a police officer in your marriage? If you insist that you don't, then I would presume that you never point out what your spouse has done wrong – right?

Why Husbands Don't Listen

Don't get me wrong, communication is important – especially for females.

But your communication is destined to be disconnecting if your conversations are all about you or the kids, or directive in nature. For example, wives often complain that their husbands don't listen. Quite often, the reason for this is because they hate to be parented or criticized by their wives.

As an illustration to convey this point, about a decade ago, my wife asked me why men experience difficulty listening to their wives. In response, I asked my wife what she would think of a woman who got into her car and, without, doing anything else, actually said to the car, *Take me to where I want to go!*

My wife's response was, *That would be pretty stupid!*

I then asked her, *What then would you think of a woman who did this every day?*

Her response was, I *believe that this person would definitely need major help. Definitely she would be need to be put on medication and, yes, I think that she would need to be institutionalized with little hope of ever getting better.*

My response to my wife was, *Do you know why that car did not take that woman to where she wanted to go?*

Yes, she replied.

I said, *The answer is quite simple: it is because the manufacturer of that car did not create the car to respond to a woman's instruction! Similarly, this is why men don't listen. In short, a man was not created to likewise respond to a woman's instruction; he was designed to respond to a woman's example!*

Quite simply, men consider it an act of disrespect when they are told what to do by their wives or when they perceive that their actions are scrutinized by their wives. Thus, a husband's natural reaction to this type of behavior is to ignore her, become defensive, resistant, critical, or contemptuous.

Being told, *You're not listening to me!* typically ignites the fuse that leads to the subsequent marital conflict or explosion if at least one of the spouses do not disengage from the discussion or give in to the directives of the other. As many times as I have asserted, *You get what you give in some form,* how can a husband's reaction not be seen as a dynamic that is initiated by his wife's complaint, lazed with a disrespectful directive – *listen*?

More specifically, for a husband, being told, *You're not listening to me!* gets translated by him to, *You are going to listen to me young man and do exactly what I say or there will be hell to pay!*

Also, please consider who benefits from being made to listen.

It is the one doing the talking!

And the longer the husband is made to listen, the more disrespected he feels.

If a husband chooses to listen to avoid an all-out marital war, is love actually being practiced by his wife?

Be honest - wouldn't you agree that whatever she has to say is primarily designed for her highest good? When she wants him to listen to something that is important to her, does he or does he not have no other option but to listen – or else?

Love in practice always seeks out the other person's highest good, not the other way around.

Love engages the person who, in turn, not only wants to listen, but to listen more! A husband being forced to listen feels about connected to his wife, as she feels connected to him after succumbing to his rants about wanting sex. In both examples, the end result is, to say the least, a disconnection of the bond and the disintegration of their marriage.

Don't get me wrong – a wife's marital needs are just as important as a husband's. But a wife's typical approach in getting her marital needs met is generally wrong. While he may comply with her request, it is basically under duress, as he would rather give in than argue for weeks. I see this communication dynamic constantly unfold in my counseling practice.

When fear wins, love loses!

Secondly, attempting to influence your husband by making him listen is an ineffective approach because men are visual. That is why they do not listen.

If you begin approaching him in the way wherein he is receptive, you will increasingly come to see a transformation take place; he will want to hear all that you have to say and will solicit your advice.

In the end, you both win! A win-win outcome is the end result of love in practice. This is what has occurred for many whom I have counseled. Once they changed their dynamic of communicating to one that conforms to love, so did the outcome of their discussion.

Gender differences account for many of the problems that develop between husbands and wives. Regarding the issue of marital communication, being auditory in their orientation, women attempt to approach a man through his ears (e.g., *You're not listening!*), as opposed to through his eyes.

Please consider that there are two basic ways to influence an individual, through promotion or attraction.

Promotion involves making your case through your words.

Attraction involves being the type of person that causes the other to gravitate toward and be responsive him or her.

Considering the fact that love only wants to give, promoting your cause or point-of-view basically conveys the message, *I want to get ...* as opposed to, *I want to give for your highest good.*

Thus, when a wife who communicates with her husband with the motive to give, as opposed to criticizing or correcting him for his shortcomings, his feelings of connectedness towards her and trust in her will grow simultaneously.

Please also be informed that lengthy communication can come across as a lecture or being self-serving if your spouse is being required to listen for long periods of time, least you be offended.

Engaging in a power struggle is the last thing a husband wants.

Why?

Because it results in him getting less marital needs met than he was prior to the discussion.

Whenever individuals get married, *Two become One.* Therefore, no one actually wins a power struggle. The couple either wins together or loses together. Therefore, when each spouse puts love into practice at the same time, they will win together. The refusal of meeting any marital need is the etiology and hallmark of poor communication.

Regardless of how nicely the need is denied, a denied marital need is an act of selfishness that poisons the pureness of the flow of love between the married couple who are *One* in every sense of the word.

Therefore, getting even is analogous to shooting yourself in the foot or committing relationship suicide.

The 15-Second Rule

It only takes 15 seconds or less to actually say what you have to say and/or to verbalize your commitment to meet your spouse's marital needs.

In fact, Frank and Lois, who are friends of my wife and I, have claimed that their marriage was saved by abiding by one of my recommendations pursuant to effective communication: Each spouse should speak to each other for up to 15 seconds and then allow the other to respond, up to 15 seconds.

Yes, the *15 Second Rule* saved my friends marriage; it can likewise save yours!

If much has to be said, each spouse should speak for up to 15 seconds and then give the other spouse an opportunity to respond.

The end result of the conversation should be a commitment of both spouse's parts to meet all of each other's marital needs unconditionally.

Therefore, an unconditional *Yes* response to a stated marital need does not warrant long-winded discussions, debates, or arguments.

Breaking the Unhealthy Communication Dynamic

If your spouse engages in self-centered or destructive communication, there are three basic ways to break this unhealthy dynamic (that can be accomplished in 15 seconds or less):

1. Do <u>not</u> reciprocate by likewise responding to your spouse with self-centered or destructive communication, such as name-calling, criticizing and the like.

2. Ask your spouse, *What is it that I need to be saying, doing, or giving to make you feel differently towards me?*

3. If you have agreed with your spouse to put the principles and recommendations cited herein into practice, remind your spouse that both of you have originally agreed to address your problems and issues in a way that conforms with putting love into practice, and that you would like to get back on track, in terms of doing that.

Gender Differences and Communication Interests

Please consider that innate gender differences may also account for your spouse's seeming indifference during your conversation. To illustrate these differences, please allow me to tell you a brief story regarding what happened not long ago at a social event my wife and I attended at a friends' house a few months ago.

As is quite typical with adult social events, the females were all congregated together and the males were likewise all congregated together.

To amuse themselves, the males began discussing what they predicted their wives were talking about.

There was quickly a consensus that their discussion was either about the kids, complaints about co-workers, health and illness or diet.

For fun, I told them that I was going to interrupt their conversation and attempt to change it to sports. The husbands all smiled and chuckled as I approached the table on the deck where their wives were seemingly having a meeting.

The topic was about health and illness.

Three times in a row over the course of 10 minutes I attempted to interject something interesting about sports and each time their discussion about someone's poor health continued.

While some of you may be thinking, *boys will be boys and girls will be girls*, my intuition about the husbands were right; they felt left out while their ongoing disappointment about their wives became evident – that is, in general, they feel that their wives show very little and certainly not enough interest in discussing their particular interests.

Men know what interests their wives. It is those things that she discusses all of the time, including the things they complain about.

Therefore, husbands know that their wives are not interested in matters that are not brought up as topics of discussion.

In the same way that the true meaning and intent is lost when a wife complains about her husband not bringing her home flowers unexpectedly as a gesture of love and, in turn, he immediately brings home flowers, having to ask her to initiate action to meet his stated marital needs likewise loses its' impact.

You may be asking, *What interests men?*

My answer is, *A much lesser dose of what interests females, combined with sports, politics, sex, hobbies, repair, history, mechanics, how to make more money, fitness, and automobiles. Men prefer to share their likes and preferences, whereas females like to share challenging sad stories, things that have irritated them in the recent past, and the status of their children.*

Some Gender Differences That Account for Couple Conflict

The following gender differences often accounts for couple conflict. Hopefully, this information will enable you to better understand your spouse and take these points into consideration when differences appear to divide you.

- Whereas wives focus on the process of communicating (such as eye contact, listening, etc.), husbands focus on the content of the communication (i.e., the message).

- Whereas wives reason relative to feelings and subjective experiences (e.g., *I do not feel like it, so I shouldn't have to!*), husbands are reason, fact, and principle-oriented.

- Whereas wives expand under stress, causing them to discuss problems and issues and solicit other's input; husbands contract or withdraw emotionally under stress. Consequently, wives inaccurately perceive their husbands being indifferent.

- Wives are more interested in the topics of love, sharing, communication, cooperation, intimacy, intuition, and harmony; husbands are more interested in producing results, achieving goals, power, competition, work, logic, and efficiency.

- Whereas wives tend to form opinions impressionistically, husbands tend to form opinions and conclusions, based upon knowledge at hand.

- To a wife, reconciliation is a process; to a husband reconciliation is an event. Thus, wives need for their feelings to be understood and to heal over time for a reconnection to occur; husbands expect that repentance and an apology should be sufficient for reconciliation to occur.

- While wives prioritize relationships, husbands tend to prioritize goals. This causes wives to have an inclination to over-focus on their children and husbands to over-focus on their jobs.

- While wives communicate to explore and share a topic, husbands communicate to simply make a point with a purpose behind it.

- For wives, emotional connectedness is needed to be responsive to sex; to the contrary, for husbands emotional connectedness is achieved through sexual initiative and responsivity of their wives.

- For wives, self-esteem is affected by the quality of her relationship; for husbands, self-esteem and his identity is affected as a result of what he does (i.e., work, sports, etc.).

- To be emotionally receptive, wives need to feel loved, valued, accepted, and understood; to be emotionally receptive, husbands need expressed admiration and to feel respected.

- Wives want their husband's unconditional love and understanding to feel secure and special; husbands desire sex unconditionally and unrestrictively to feel love and respected.

- Whereas wives are turned off by insensitivity and indifference, husbands are turned off by rehashing, interrogation, and criticism.

- Whereas wives need to feel that her needs, wishes, and desires are respected, husbands need to hear their wives' genuine appreciation of his support and provisions for the family.

- Whereas wives feel that a connection is achieved through love, husbands perceive that a connection is achieved through admiration.

- Whereas wives desired to being treated "special," (i.e., receiving symbols of love, such as flowers, love notes, cards, etc.), husbands desire to be treated in high regard, such as being served, making the final decision, and the like.

The Mid-Ground for Disparities between Husbands and Wives

In consideration of gender differences, you may be asking, *What is the mid-ground for the disparity among the sexes?*

The answer to this is quite easy and may sound over-simplistic: For each spouse to discuss their likes and marital needs, abiding by "the 15 Second Rule."

As such, if husbands and wives are putting love into practice, each will be considering the needs and interests of their spouses above their own and a balance in their discussions will be the end result. In addition, communication will be enjoyable and engaging.

Incidentally, does your spouse typically just sit there like a *bump on a log*?

Unless you are the extreme rare exception, it is most likely because you have shown not enough interest in the things he or she enjoys or because you are too negative or critical.

If you are engaging, your spouse will likewise become engaging.

You can do this in 15 seconds or less.

The alternative is a co-existent marriage.

Incidentally, are you feeling uneasy, slightly irritable, or defensive?

If you are, by this time, you should know why.

The Story of Ed and Cindy. The impact of communicating with a husband in a manner that he is most responsive can best be exemplified by the response of a husband in a recent couple's counseling session. At the beginning of the session, the wife directly confronted me for making her feel left out in the prior session. During various parts of this session, the husband and I shared our thoughts about the football playoffs, as well as how to best build muscle mass.

Nevertheless, my bond with the husband was solidified by our discussion, as was evidenced by the fact that he agreed to do repair work in the house that he had resisted making for 20 years.

In this regard, the wife exclaimed, *I have been trying to get my husband to do repairs in our house for 20 years and, in less than 20 minutes, you were able to get him to do it! What did you just do?!*

My response was, *Do you remember just telling me how I made you feel left out last session? I was establishing the foundation to what your husband just agreed to do.*

In effect, in some form, I got what I gave!

If you want to break through an impasse with your spouse, simply relate to him or her on his or her terms and in a manner that generates receptivity and you will reap what you sow. When you do, don't be surprised if you get the response you are hoping for in 15 seconds or less! If you don't, you may likewise be waiting for your need to get met for 20 years or longer.

Guidelines for Effective Marital Communication

The communication guidelines below are based on a handout that I give every married couple for the purpose of managing their communication. You will be putting these guidelines into practice automatically as you put love into practice in your marriage by saying and doing those things that you know will make your spouse as happy as possible.

1. Speak one at a time, without interrupting.

2. Always keep your volume at a normal level, without being defensive.

3. Listen, and attempt to fully understand your spouse's point-of-view.

4. Get rid of your negative attitude! Remember, the difference between a disagreement and an argument is the presence of a negative attitude.

5. Stay on one topic at a time. Do not introduce new topics till the one at hand is resolved, wherein you both have attained a win-win outcome.

6. State your purpose for wanting to speak, and assure your partner that you are interested in hearing his or her and arriving at a win-win solution.

7. Always answer your spouse's questions without counterattacking.

8. If you disagree, please state that you disagree when it is your turn to talk.

9. Always show respect for your spouse's different point-of-view, even when you do not agree with it. Practice the *Golden Rule*; love your spouse like yourself!

10. Say what you have to say in **15 seconds or less**; then invite your spouse to respond.

11. Refrain from name-calling, cursing, giving dirty looks, or characterizing your spouse. Rather, validate your spouse so you will be in a better position to request it.

12. Only attempt to discuss critical issues when both you and your spouse are rested and in a fairly good mood. Never attempt to force your partner into discussing a matter.

13. Do not attempt to discuss critical issues while under the influence of alcohol or drugs.

14. Do not seek support for your position from outside parties, including your children and parents, for the purpose of proving your spouse wrong.

15. Apologize when you realize that you have engaged in destructive communication, and always be willing to accept your spouse's apology.

16. Stop discussing the same topic over and over again.

17. Never use your feelings of being victimized as a justification for not putting forth your best effort in attempting to work-through a particular problem.

18. Refrain from using the phrases, *You always!* or *You never!*

19. While "silence is golden," remember that the silent treatment is being passive-aggressive, in the same way that withholding is passive-aggressive.

20. Never make threats or evaluative statements, such as *You'll never change!*

21. Never become defensive when your spouse is articulating his or her point-of-view.

22. Never provide your position without letting your spouse know that you understand his or her different point-of-view.

23. Practice understanding and interest, rather than defensiveness and rebuttal.

24. Even though you may believe that your spouse is wrong, please attempt to see your part in the conflict, and the changes that both of you need to make for achieving a win-win solution. Be clear and specific as to what the solution is to you.

25. Your communication should always reflect patience, understanding, respect, and consideration for your spouse's opinion and feelings.

Unfortunately, most of the couples I counsel refer to this list only when they are getting along with each other.

These communication tools are like construction tools in that they are only useful, to the degree that you use them when they are needed.

Hopefully, you will refer to and use this list when you perceive that the communication dynamics between you and your spouse are becoming unmanageable.

Ideally, you will come to a point where you do not need to refer to this list because you are consistently putting love into practice in your marriage and following the blueprint herein for your marriage miracle.

I inform every one of my couples in counseling that this list will ultimately come to be unnecessary to refer to as they put love into actual practice in their marriage.

Why?

Because putting into practice these communication tips become automatic when you shift your thinking *from the get to the give* and, consequently, be totally concerned with your spouse's highest good and total happiness, as opposed to what you haven't been getting.

Chapter 6

Marriage Miracle Instructions to Wives

At this point, you may still be struggling with skepticism regarding the notion or premise that you can literally have a transformed or the perfect marriage in 15 seconds or less.

For your benefit, this book offers proven solutions to your marital problems and issues that can indeed be generated in 15 seconds or less.

As an illustration, let's pretend that a very rich person pulled your name from a hat and, in turn, you became the winner of one hundred billion dollars.

Wouldn't you agree that this amount of money would solve all of your financial concerns and make it possible for you to pay off all of your bills and purchase things that would satisfy your dreams, at least from a materialistic perspective?

With this money, let's suppose that one of your dreams was to design a 10,000 square foot home with every conceivable detail of it conforming to your liking. Although you have more than enough money to build your dream house, it will still take time to actually design it, select the types and grades of materials of your choice, etc.

Regarding your dream marriage, you have at hand what you need to construct the marriage of your dreams ... and it only takes 15 seconds or less to begin the process!

Unfortunately, most resist making the changes that are required to make this a reality, even though the answers are at their finger tips.

Using the *dream house illustration* as an example, they resist doing what is necessary in designing their dream house because it takes effort.

In effect, if their dream house doesn't fall from the sky and land exactly in the location they want it to be, they aren't interested.

Putting forth effort in making a few needed, but profound changes, is simply too much to expect. This prideful self-centered attitude of entitlement is at the heart of every relationship problem.

I don't have to make any changes because my husband is the bad guy and I don't feel like doing what pleases him, is the prevailing mindset of most marriages that are stuck in the mud (on the wife's side of the marital equation).

Is this your attitude?

If it is, you have no right to complain.

To obtain your marriage miracle, your focus should be on what you need to be giving your spouse, as opposed to being disgruntled about what you have not been getting from him.

Proof That Your Marriage Miracle is At Hand

In this illustration, I will prove that the answer for your marriage miracle is but 15 seconds or less away.

In fact, you are about to prove me right!

Are you ready?

Let's pretend that, as my client, I just met you and your husband and have listened to each of your complaints about each other. In response, I request that your husband step out into my waiting room in order to speak with you in private.

You and I are now alone in my office. At this point, I ask you to take a few moments to identify your children (if you are a parent) or identify someone that you love dearly (if you are not a parent). In this case, let's assume that you are a parent. There is no doubt in my mind that you would be willing to die for your children. Wouldn't you agree?

Subsequently, let's pretend that I immediately turn into a demon that has the power to kill at will. Then I look at you with a sinister and contemptuous demeanor and exclaim:

You have until midnight to accomplish the task of capturing your husband's heart completely or you will never see your child (or children) again!

To prove my evil intent, I pick up the phone and allow you to hear your child(ren) cry, *Mommy, mommy, please don't let them hurt me! Help me, help me, mommy!*

Immediately, I point my finger in your face and say, *"Don't worry, the torture will not begin until midnight, but it will only occur if your husband feels connected to you less than 100%!" I have the ability to look within your husband's heart and determine the degree to which he feels connected to you, from 0% to 100%.*

The condition for saving the lives of your children is simple: Say or do what is necessary to give of yourself to capture your husband's heart completely – 100% - nothing less!

Without turning the page, please take 15 seconds or less to answer the following question: <u>What you would say, do, or give in order to accomplish capturing your husband's heart completely by midnight?</u>

<u>Very important consideration!:</u> Be totally honest. Honesty is vital to your marriage miracle. Until you have answered this question please do <u>not</u> read ahead.

****

Wouldn't you agree with me that what you would say, do, or give would basically fall into 2 major categories: <u>expressed admiration</u> and <u>sexual fulfillment</u>?

I know that this is your answer.

Under these conditions, would you deny any of your husband's requests?

I'm sure that you would say, *No.*

<u>Please consider what your answers would be to the following questions:</u>

- Would your total focus be on what love requires, that is, giving of yourself completely with the goal of making him as happy as possible?

I'm sure you would say, *Yes.*

- Would you use your feelings, your husband's past behaviors, your energy level, your own desires, or any other justification to risk not making your husband completely happy and fulfilled?

    I'm sure you would say, *No.*

- Would you express anger towards your husband, even if he was mean or inconsiderate?

    I'm sure you would say, *No.*

- Would you compare your husband to anyone else regarding him falling short of your expectations?

    I'm sure you would say, *No.*

- Would you critique, question, or criticize the way he disciplines the children?

    I'm sure you would say, *No.*

- Would you support all of your husband's decisions?

    I'm sure you would say, *Yes.*

- What topic areas would you discuss with your husband?

    I'm sure that you would basically say, *The one's that interest him the most.*

<u>Quick Note</u>: Now don't forget that your children's lives depend on your capturing your husband's heart completely by midnight!

- Would you complain about anything?

    I'm sure you would say, *No.*

- Would you be the one who initiated sex?

    I'm sure you would say, *Yes.*

    And if he wanted to "swing from the chandelier," wouldn't you happily say, *Yes!*?

    Of course you would! ☺

Need I ask you any specific questions regarding your willingness to make your husband 100% happy in this area of your marriage?

Well, let's see.

- What if your husband said that he believes the moon is made of green cheese? Would you disagree with him, even though you have a much different opinion?

    I'm sure that you would unhesitantly agree with him, if asked.

- Would you go out of your way to point out all of his positive attributes?

    I'm sure that you would say, *Yes.*

- Would you bring up anything negative from the past?

    I'm sure that you would say, *No.*

- Would you attempt to negotiate or reach any compromises with your husband?

    I'm sure that you would say, *No.*

Wouldn't you agree with me that you didn't need to read any book or consult anyone else to know exactly how to please your husband completely and capture his heart?

… and that you, without hesitation, knew the answers to every one of these questions?

I'm sure that you would say, *Yes.*

Therefore, would you now agree with me, that your ability to love is innate and doesn't have to be negotiated, communicated effectively, or figured out by a therapist or a clergyman?

So why are you feeling disappointed and, to some degree, defensive at this point?

You should feel relieved, liberated and victorious; you have your answer! And you need not have to think beyond 15 seconds to put your answer into use at any given point or time! Thus, if you make the needed changes, by the end of the day you will be reaping what you have been giving! And it's all good, because it involves putting love into actual practice.

You can now fire your therapist or at least take a break from your couple's counseling.

While your husband may be skeptical at first to some degree in response to your miraculous changes, he will nevertheless be overcome by the wonder and power of your love.

You should be saying to yourself at this moment, *This is wonderful; I finally get it! And, Dr. Racite is right; it only takes 15 seconds or less to make up my mind to have the marriage of my dreams!*

But I doubt that this is what you are actually thinking – at least completely.

Rather, you are still struggling with doubt and fear to a certain degree, while fighting off those internalized antithetical messages regarding love that are at the root of every co-existent and failing marriage. Please, let it go! Let love be your guiding force, not fear.

You may also be handicapped with false pride and indignation, causing you to be tempted to dismiss the message of this book and redefine its' core message as, in effect, a promotion of co-dependency, slavery, subservience, being a doormat, and adopting a "Stepford Wife" mentality and disposition to conform to other's distorted way of thinking about love, resulting in a dismantlement of your innate value system.

You have everything to gain, but nothing to lose by embracing and practicing love – true love!

Please also consider that your internalized misinterpretation of love from others, as something that has to be deserved to be given, conflicts with the spirit and letter of your marriage vows. In this regard, you vowed to love 100% in the same way you vowed to be faithful 100%. Any contrary view will result in a misguided cafeteria-style marital arrangement that ensures a co-existent or unhappy marriage and most likely a future divorce.

Moreover, if you are struggling with the thought that meeting your husband's marital needs completely and unconditionally is unfair, did you not say, *to love, to honor, to cherish* etc. before you said, *I do*?

You unconditionally vowed, *to be faithful* 100% of the time, whether you feel like it or not. This entitles your husband to fidelity regardless of his actions. Similarly, he is entitled to the fulfillment of the other vows, regardless of his actions.

Therefore, please consider, determine, and change why are you struggling to any degree with the thought of completely fulfilling the other vows, as opposed to dismantling them with an, *if I feel like it,* contingency. For once, be controlled and guided by love, not immobilizing and destructive fear. Love will see you through your marital difficulties, whereas fear will keep you and your spouse stuck and perpetually unhappy.

The "Capture Effect"

Your innate knowledge regarding how to capture your husband's heart completely, will produce what I term, *The Capture Effect*, if you put it into actual practice.

The *Capture Effect* is the effect that a husband must feel in order to be the most responsive and receptive in the marital relationship. This is met primarily through expressed admiration and sexual fulfillment. [5]

Most women assert that men are "all ego" and only care about "one thing." Then they act surprised when this comes to pass! Moreover, they actually spend a lifetime attempting to change these dispositions.

Please think about the negative message this conveys to husbands, especially yours!

A Husband's Greatest Marital Need: Expressed Admiration

A husband's greatest marital need is to be admired unconditionally. To a husband, admiration is love. Expressed admiration is putting love into action.

A synonym that most closely depicts admiration is the word, *respect.*

Some synonyms for *respect* include the following words: *highly regarded, honor, favor, value, exalt, revere,* and *deference.*

For this marital need to be met, it must be unconditionally expressed and exhibited.

The following are ways to meet your husband's marital need for expressed admiration:

1. Making positive comments to him when he feels discouraged.

2. Not undermining or questioning his household rules for the children or consequences for their misbehavior or noncompliance.

3. Refraining from bringing up his past or present shortcomings, unless requested by him.

4. Refraining from saying and doing things that he finds pleasing.

5. Not offering him unsolicited advice or suggestions (as this is perceived as direct or veiled criticism).

6. Treating him and speaking to him in a manner that is "fitting to a King."

7. Not disagreeing with him or contradicting him, unless he explicitly asks for your opinion.

8. Not exhibiting defensiveness or feelings of victimization regarding his past or current actions or decisions.

9. Meeting all of his marital needs (e.g., recreational companionship, sexual fulfillment, domestic support, respect for his leadership as a parent etc.) as a priority, "with complete heart" and a sense of urgency.

Yes, your "ego-maniac" husband wants to be treated like and perceived as a King!

Wouldn't these recommendations be automatic if your children's lives depended upon you capturing your husband's heart completely?

Of course, you innately know the answer!

However, what confuses me is why you have neglected to make this a reality – to make the necessary changes that will prompt him to feel "connected" to you.

After all, haven't you essentially already asserted that your husband would feel completely connected to you if you treated him with unconditional expressed admiration?

Perhaps your mental wires are crossed, in terms of what you know deep down in your gut, with the contrasting messages you have received throughout a lifetime that have directed you to exhibit the exact opposite.

Do you feel wonderful about how liberated you have become during the course of your marriage? You know … being your own person and not being "controlled" by your demanding and inconsiderate husband?

Yes, liberated but unhappy, or liberated and headed for divorce or already divorced, while all of the time, your marriage miracle was right at your finger tips.

However, the great news is that you are now but 15 seconds away from tapping into marital bliss. But what direction will you now choose?

Please choose 100% love!

Research Supporting a Husband's Need for Admiration

In his book, *The Seven Principles for Making Marriage Work*, Dr. John Gottman recommends fondness and admiration to be exhibited. [6]

Moreover, he revisited the findings from his 120+ research-based studies on couples to determine the core issue to all marital difficulties.

Dr. Gottman found that **the common ingredient in all forms of marital discord was the husband's negative reaction to his wife's attempts at control.**

A husband's negative reaction can take the form of either flight (e.g., emotional distancing) or fight (e.g., arguing and being mean-spirited). [7]

The implication of Dr. Gottman's research findings is astounding, and supports my recommendations, along with the 9 recommendations provided herein.

For one moment, please consider whether you would conclude that giving up control is essential for capturing your husband's heart completely by the end of the day if your children's lives were at risk if you did not. You know the answer.

Also, in order to determine the extent that you fall short of meeting your husband's marital needs, simply ask your husband to make believe that he has a magic wand, and make a wish regarding any marital need that is not completely met to his total satisfaction.

If you are serious about attaining your *marriage miracle*, this is a must!

Are you feeling that the recommendations that are given herein are one-sided?

I know that you are.

However, once you totally believe that love, rather than withholding, is the answer, you will also increasingly come to see that you will get what you give. In this regard, simply give him control and, much faster than you anticipate, your husband will be soliciting your advice and doing whatever he can to meet your needs and make you happy!

Go ahead. Put my recommendations to the test. The very few that have chosen to love, as opposed to embrace fear, have not been disappointed. Perhaps your resistance is rooted in issues that have nothing to do with him. I am saying this is because individuals have a tendency to reenact issues in their relationships that they have not resolved from the past.

In any event, what should make you the happiest is making him happy by meeting all of his marital needs.

And, as a spouse who pledged to love your husband completely, why would you ever consider meeting any of his marital needs as unreasonable, an annoyance, or a sacrifice?

In reality, it is unfair and audacious for you to ever feel that your husband has nerve in expecting you to please him. And, of course, the same applies to him as well.

Exhibit Faith in Him

To those wives who embrace Biblical teachings regarding marriage, I liken a husband's greatest marital need to what pleases God the most. In this regard, the Bible states in *Hebrews 11:6* that *without faith it is impossible to please God.*

Men are no different.

Thus, without exhibiting unconditional faith (or exhibited confidence) in your husband, you cannot please him.

Do you hear me? Without exhibiting unconditional faith in your husband you cannot please him!

Before you assume that you have faith in your husband, please examine some of the indications below which exemplify that you do:

- Not offering unsolicited advice or suggestions, no matter how helpful.

- Being happy, confident, and satisfied with all of his decisions.

- Not taking issue with him wanting to be the leader of the marital home.

- Not interfering with or critiquing his attempts at disciplining the children.

- Demonstrating the qualities of a virtuous wife towards him.

It is very difficult for me to convince wives of the extremely negative impact that offering unsolicited advice has upon a husband's perception of getting his greatest marital need of admiration met. In support of Dr. Gottman's research findings, their need to control frequently gets in the way of meeting this need. It is indeed an issue of control because there wouldn't ever be any arguments if the issue of control was not present. As a manifestation of your faith in him, you would experience contented agreement with your husband.

In fact, Dr. Gottman's research on married couples found that, more than 80 percent of the time, wives are the ones who bring up *sticky marital issues*, while their husbands try to avoid discussing them, presumably to avoid an argument and power struggle. [8]

If you are feeling defensive or upset with the notion that I am promoting a "male-dominated household," you are missing the whole point!

The point is that love is the answer. Love takes the form of giving. The goal of love is the other person's highest good. The need to embrace and/or insist in your husband abiding to your point-of-view attests to your focus on your highest good, resulting from your fear that your husband's decisions will fall short of achieving it.

The need to "get your two cents in" is evidence of your lack of faith and need to control.

And be honest – do you get upset when you don't get your own way, but your husband does?

An individual with a heart of love should find the greatest amount of pleasure in seeing the other person happy. Having faith in your husband will result in the assurance that your loved-based actions will surely be reciprocated.

Yes, the same standard applies to your husband. But the point of this chapter is to give you direction regarding what you, not him, need to do for your marriage miracle.

Regarding the specific recommendations provided herein, you may have developed the mindset that you and, in fact, all women are being bashed. Hopefully, you have not developed this mindset.

If you have truly internalized the central message herein of the power of 100% love and practice it, you will quickly see that the manifestation of the promise of this message - love never fails.

Therefore, when you meet your husband's greatest marital need, through exhibiting admiration, including the requirement of not offering unsolicited advice, you can be assured that the faith that you have exhibited in him will be reciprocated. In response to your support and deference to his needs, he will have faith in you and, in turn, solicit your advice and, almost always, do whatever pleases you; it's that simple! You will get what you give!

In many marriages, husbands are "gun shy" and emotionally shut down from past arguments, regarding their attempts to make decisions and simply be themselves. Consequently, they exhibit what is known as, *learned helplessness* in the mental health field. Thus, once you decide to convey a "green light" to your husband, with respect to making various decisions and, in doing so, consistently relinquishing your need to control, he may continue for some time in his pattern of simply doing nothing or not taking the initiative.

This is where your expressed admiration, reassurance, and encouragement are vital – especially when he makes a decision that he knows or assumes is in opposition to your point-of-view. So many wives complain about their husband's lack of initiative, but then complain or provide their unsolicited input when he makes attempts at managing the home affairs. The husband who is a "coach potato" is an excellent example of the effects of an over-controlling wife whose lack of faith in her husband has him perpetually shut down.

Are you getting defensive again or prompted to disagree with me? I think you are.

But you don't know my husband, you may be screaming to yourself; *everything I do is for him and he continues to live in his own world!*

Well, perhaps this is true to some degree. After all, isn't it true that *men are from Mars and women are from Venus?*

However, gender differences should be magnets, not considered as vices.

Nevertheless, despite all of your well-meaning intentions, please allow me to provide you with some additional reasons why not exhibiting faith in your husband, as evidenced by your need to get your own way or provide unsolicited advice or direction, keeps him and the marriage stuck somewhere up in a distant location, such as in the Arctic, as opposed to a location closely approaching Florida.

In addition, it also shortchanges you from benefiting from a husband who has matured as a man and developed into all he can be and would become.

- It demonstrates your lack of confidence in his abilities and sends him the message that he is below an acceptable standard.

- It depicts your underlying belief that his decision-making is not good enough.

- It immobilizes him in all areas of the marriage, including the raising of the children.

- It prevents and often handicaps him from developing his leadership and parenting abilities.

- It causes him to become defensive, oppositional, distant, withdrawn, indifferent, and argumentative.

- It makes him very unhappy and unfulfilled as a spouse.

- It conveys an, *I don't love you for you,* message to him.

- It makes him feel like he is married to a mother, as opposed to a wife.

- It thwarts his natural emotional bonding and intimacy with you.

- It promotes the reciprocation of a lack of trust and faith that is represented by your need to provide him with well-meaning, but detrimental unsolicited advice.

- It makes him feel challenged, as opposed to successful in attending to your needs.

- It thwarts his spiritual initiative because any attempts by him to point out scriptures that direct wives to be submissive to their husbands and not give him instruction are potential triggers for severe marital conflict if they are brought to your attention.

- A husband is not "wired" to be responsive to his wife's advice; he is wired to be responsive to her example.

- It encourages him to challenge you because he feels challenged.

- It creates a, *me against you,* mindset.

- It greatly thwarts his initiative, while contributing to his mobilization.

How many more reasons do you need to make the commitment to meet your husband's greatest marital need of being admired through your expressed faith in him?

Exhibit the Qualities of the Proverbs 31 (Virtuous) Wife

The qualities that God desires for wives to exhibit are found in the Old Testament in *Proverbs 31: 10-31.* The *Proverbs 31 wife* is referred to as *the virtuous wife.*

If these qualities are advocated by God, they are certainly worthy of mentioning for attaining your *marriage miracle.*

The virtuous wife:

- Is a woman of mental, physical, and spiritual strength.

- Is not weak, dependent, emotionally reactive, idle, or frail.

- Is a rare treasure in her husband's life.

- Is worth more than rubies because she is of such great value.

- Brings the color, the love, the joy, the energy, and the life to the home.

- Causes her husband to never have to worry about her character, her emotional reactions, her management of the home, and how she handles her finances and time.

- Possesses qualities, attributes, and the character that enable her to be her husband's backbone.

- Is intent on lavishing every possible good upon her husband everyday.

- Does her husband good at every opportunity, and routinely operates her life and home in a way that benefits her husband with good.

- Exhibits actions that are designed to love, serve, honor, advance, encourage, and support her husband, while easing his life in every way possible.

- Does not expect any payoff or reward for pleasing her husband.

- While at home, works with her hands willingly, cheerfully, delightfully, creatively, and diligently.

- Is motivated with a heart of love to go the extra mile to meet the needs of her husband and the household.

- Possesses a visionary mind, initiative, and good judgment in the act of carefully choosing what is in the long-term best interests of her family.

- Allows her mind to control her heart and, in doing so, carefully analyzes a situation before acting.

- Embraces an unwavering commitment to work and a standard of excellence.

- Harnesses her energy and prepares herself for the tasks at hand in a manner that results in her being able to overcome adversities, distractions and unforeseen obstacles.

- Is ever-persevering and continuously industrious, even into the evening.

- Exhibits a cheerful attitude, for her heart delights in pleasing her husband.

- Responds to opportunities to help others that are less fortunate and, in doing so, reaches out to others in need as far as her means will allow.

- Possesses a heartfelt desire to provide more than is sufficient to meet the needs of all of those residing in her household.

- Never neglects to meet her husband's marital needs.

- Is continuously intent in being the best wife possible and in making her home an environment that is fitting for a king.

- Supports her husband in such a way that leads to his success and influence in the world.

- Is a crown to her husband, due to her devoted support and demonstrated honor to him.

- Adorns herself with the clothing of strength and dignity with a quaint demeanor, representing the virtues of a godly character.

- Exhibits her internal strength and godly character in a number of ways, such as her exhibiting a quiet and gentle spirit, wisdom, perseverance, dignified conduct, deference and respect for her husband, support for her husband's plans and goals, and trust in God for facilitating whatever changes her husband needs to make to fulfill his potential and be the best husband possible.

- Is kind and speaks with wisdom, controlling the words that come out of her mouth and refraining from saying anything that her husband would consider as being dishonorable.

- Wisely refrains from being contentious.

- Trusts that her chaste conduct and prayerful support of her husband will prompt God to intercede on her behalf if he is wrong, unreasonable, or neglectful of his duties as a husband and father.

- Regardless of the circumstances, maintains her role as a faithful wife who is responsive to her husband's marital needs and God's statutes.

- Exercises single-mindedness in doing what is pleasing to her husband, even when her husband is not doing what God expects.

- Exhibits actions and emotional reactions, in accordance with what is dictated by what God expects, as opposed to her perceptions and feelings.

- Being always alert and energetic, she carefully notices the patterns and habits of all who reside with her home.

- Is always very productive, while holding her children to a high standard in developing their potential and fulfilling their responsibilities.

- Focuses her efforts in raising her children to love, honor, and serve God.

- Captivates her husband by her excellencies wherein he consequently views her as the "best among the best."

- Focuses most of her attention on her inner character instead of her external appearance.

- Exhibits inner beauty with respect to initiative, practices, principles, and how she responds when her husband does not fulfill her expectations.

- Views obeying God and making her husband happy as rewards in and of themselves.

- Does not seek praise for her actions. However, it is given as a natural result of her orientation, demeanor, role model, and being pleasing in God's sight.

Doesn't this say it all?

After examining the content of this section, I contemplated, *Should I have claimed to have written a unique message? God has already set the standards for attaining, the perfect marriage.*

Do these qualities of virtue conform to what you have by taught by others?

The Impact of Treating Your Husband With Admiration

Please keep in mind that the end result of treating your husband as a King will be reciprocated by him in the form of treating you as a Queen.

The marital, *To Honor,* vow entitles you to be treated like a Queen. Therefore, please trust that it is my motive to help you to and, figuratively speaking, elevate your status from a wife to a Queen.

Please don't denigrate or shortchange yourself by acting in a less elevated way than a Queen. Please keep in mind that a Queen is dignified. She is perceived by others in accordance with how she acts and conducts herself. All too often, wives exhibit self-defeating behaviors by allowing themselves to lose emotional control or retaliate for their perception of being mistreated by their husbands. Standing toe-to-toe with your husband may get him to back-off, but it will do nothing to capture his heart or to respect you. You must change your method to conform to your marital vows for there to be any hope for a happy and mutually-fulfilling marriage.

When tempers are not flaring, simply ask your husband what would motivate him the most and make him the happiest, and I can assure you that you will begin wondering whether he has memorized the Proverbs 31 list of behaviors that you have been provided herein.

Moreover, allowing your children to be disobedient and disrespectful to your husband, "the King," is very unbecoming and will make him feel degraded more than anything else.

In effect, what you permit, by undermining or critiquing your husband when the children are misbehaving, is what you are promoting when you do this.

More than anything else, your children need to see loving role models, as well as to learn respect, accountability, and responsibility.

Criticizing or correcting your husband for his attempts to discipline your children is analogous to demoting him from a King to a status below a servant. You will never capture his heart if you, in effect, continue to require your husband to *bow down* to you and your kids; he will never feel admired.

If you care enough, you will ask your husband about his perception or how he is treated in this area and then make necessary changes. Otherwise, I can assure you that everyone will lose out … and, yes, it will be your fault!

I guarantee you that your children will attempt to triangulate you against your husband by managing to successfully play the victim role or in making you fear that you will lose their love forever if you do not cave-in to their demands.

Any healthy home should have explicit expectations and explicit consequences … and any rule is as effective as it is enforced.

If you believe that your husband's consequences are "extreme," chances are great that you still have little hope for a happy marriage and a husband who feels admired and believes that you have faith in him.

Coercing your husband into counseling as a means of finding an advocate for your position will simply reinforce his mindset that he doesn't measure up and that your admiration for him only goes as far as your agreement with him. This is why most men resist the idea of entering into counseling.

Also, please keep in mind that a King has a much higher status than a boss. Many of you who work treat your boss with much more respect and regard than your husband. In the same way that respectful behavior is expected at the work place, your spouse is much more entitled to receive it in your home.

There is also a link between your sexual responsivity to your husband with his perception of being admired. In this regard, husbands reason their wives' sexual interest in this way: *What a woman admires is what she desires.* That is, your husband will be assured that you admire him if you show him that you desire him.

Expressed disinterest in this second most important need of a husband is tantamount to "relationship suicide" because it will surely kill his marital spirit. It represents rejection of him, the abandonment of the, *To have and to hold,* marital vow, and complete disregard for his feelings and sexual needs.

A number of years ago, I conducted sexual research on men to determine husbands' sexual needs and how they feel when these needs are not completely met. What I did not expect was the finding that nearly all of the husbands surveyed indicated that what upset them the most was their wives not initiating sex at least one-half of the time.

Lack of sexual initiative made husbands feel that they were no more than a paycheck and that their feelings and needs were not important. It amazes and equally alarms me about how often husbands, who are unfulfilled with the lack of sex in their marriages, are shut down emotionally.

The natural repercussion is that their wives become shortchanged in getting their primary marital needs met.

My finding about the impact of wives not initiating sex, as often as their husbands would like, was followed by their wives making them feel bad about the frequency by which they desired to have sex.

Research findings consistently point to sexual fulfillment as a very high marital need for husbands. It carries a great deal of weight, in terms of how he perceives that he is regarded and loved.

Please be reminded again, yes again, about what you would say, do, and give if your children's lives depended upon it.

Unless this area of your marriage changes, from where it is, to satisfying your husband 100% and 100% of the time (just as you expect your husband to do in the area of marital fidelity), you are providing a major obstacle to what is required for that intimate connection and also depriving yourself of your marriage miracle.

Are you ready to make the needed changes now?

Take 15 seconds or less – make the change!

The Stuck Couple With The Sticky Floor

Treating your husband like a King is also an attitude and orientation characterized by a willingness to unconditionally meet all of his marital needs with a passionate sense of urgency and in a heartfelt way that is exemplified by a pleasing demeanor.

An example of the impact of treating a husband with high regard occurred with one of my past couples in a counseling session a number of years ago. [9] This strong-willed and adversarial couple typifies the interactional pattern of many marriages – perhaps yours, as well.

This couple came into couple's counseling with an unresolved conflict that developed from a course of events that had occurred the day before.

In terms of background, the husband had a power-washing business and his wife assisted him by doing all of the bookkeeping and administrative paperwork at home, while she attended to their three children.

The husband was a verbally abusive and driven perfectionist, as well as an admitted sex addict who demanded sex daily and frequently from his wife.

The conflict began when the husband arrived home the day before, walked through the door, and noticed something sticky beneath his feet.

Before he left for work earlier that day, he has given his wife a written list of 15 tasks to complete.

The following dialogue occurred between this married couple when the husband returned home later that day:

Husband and Wife Dialogue:

Husband: *Honey, there is something sticky on the floor.*

Wife: *There is something sticky on the floor? Well, I had no idea that there was anything on the floor! I've been killing myself and working like a dog all day, doing the 15 things that you gave me*

	to do – and I'm still attempting to complete #14. You just walk through the door and give me orders. You don't walk in and say, "Hello," or say that you have missed me. Instead, you come in and pile more work on me. Well, I'm not your slave. You have two arms and two legs; you clean up the sticky mess!
Husband:	*Hey, I don't like your attitude! All I said was …*
Wife:	(Interrupting) *Well, I don't like your attitude either!*
Husband:	*Listen, you know what you can do!*
Wife:	*Yea, and you know what you can do too. Listen, I'm sick of you and your demands and …*
Husband:	(Interrupting) *Listen, I'm sick and tired of your attitude. I'm out of here; I don't have to put up with anymore of your …*
	(husband walks out of the house)

When this couple came to the counseling session, they had not spoken to each other since the incident. But the tension between them was quite evident.

After the wife told me what happened, she exclaimed, *Dr. Racite, you have to help us. Nothing works. You'll have to do a miracle to help us fix this!*

My response was, *Are you absolutely sure that you want me to tell you exactly what is necessary to get your miracle and you won't get offended by my recommendation?*

Her response was, *Yes!*

My response was, *Okay, I believe that I can be of help. In fact, I believe that I can provide you with an answer for your miracle. In fact, if you will simply listen and comply with my recommendation, I believe that you will have your spouse wrapped right around your little finger. In addition, you will not have to make any requests; it will be his idea. Third, he will be glad to do it and, lastly, he will not require sex in exchange.*

Oh, you have got to be kidding, Dr. Racite!, she exclaimed.

At that point, I asked the husband whether he would be receptive to me offering a recommendation that would generate this type of response in him.

His answer was, *Sure … my idea? She keeps her big mouth shut? I'm glad to do it? Sex? I want nothing to do with her!*

The following is the dialogue between myself and the wife that followed:

Dr. Racite: *In an exaggerated and dramatized example, may I show you how to capture your husband's heart in the situation that occurred yesterday between you and your husband?*

Wife: *Sure, I've got to hear what this is. Go ahead; I'm listening.*

Dr. Racite: *Okay, your husband has just come in and has pointed out to you that there is something sticky on the floor. In essence, this is what your response should be:*

Dr. Racite **(playing the role of wife):** *Hello, Honey! It's wonderful to see you. Sweetheart, I had no idea that there was anything sticky on the floor or I would have cleaned it up. I know how hard you work and I really appreciate it. I want more than anything for you to come home to a neat and clean house. Honey, had I saw the sticky mess, I would have cleaned it up immediately. But I was very busy throughout the day, trying to finish the 15 tasks you gave me to do. In fact, I'm on #14. Sweetheart, would you like me to stop what I'm doing and clean the mess or would you prefer that I finish what you have given me to do and then clean up the mess? It doesn't make a difference to me – whatever makes you the happiest!*

Dr. Racite: **(Speaking to the Husband):** *If your wife actually said those exact words to you, in response to your observation that there was something sticky on the floor, what would you do?*

Husband: *Oh, I would clean up the floor myself!*

Dr. Racite: **(Looking at the Wife):** *Are you telling me that she would have you wrapped right around your finger in that she wouldn't have to make a request, that it would be your idea, that you would be glad to do it, and that you wouldn't want sex in exchange?*

Husband: *Yes, this is what I have been telling her our entire marriage, but she has an attitude problem!*

Since I saw this couple in 1990, I have on numerous occasions asked husbands what they would do if their wife responded to them in the way that I recommended to this wife. In my professional experience, never once has a husband ever said that he would expect his wife to clean up the mess if she responded in the manner that I presented. The universal principle, *you will get what you give*, applies here.

The moment a husband feels treated like a King, a transformation takes place; he transforms into a servant! *Honey, don't worry about it; I'll clean up the mess!*

Expressed admiration motivates a man to the maximum and brings out traits in him that may seemingly require a miracle for them to become manifest.

Love does produce miracles.

I just gave you an example of one. The dialogue that I recommended to my client, the wife, took 15 seconds or less to convey.

Based upon the simple act of your will, your *15 seconds or less marriage miracle* is just ahead!

Chapter 7

Marriage Miracle Instructions to Husbands

I'm sure that you will agree with me that a wife's marital needs are a bit more complex than a husband's marital needs. This chapter is designed to help you understand them much better.

In order to succinctly answer the question of how to capture a woman's heart, I once asked my wife the following question, *In one word, how can a man capture a woman's heart?*

Her answer was, *Connect.*

I then began to inquire as to how a husband could "connect" with his wife. Her answer was, *Just show her that you love her.*

My wife's answers correspond to what I have found to be the essence of how to capture a woman's heart.

Research Supporting Primary Marital Needs

Scientific research has confirmed that love and respect are the core components to a successful marriage. After studying couples over the course of twenty years, Dr. John Gottman from the Department of Psychology at the University of Washington found that a strong undercurrent of two basic ingredients: love and respect. [10]

Dr. Emerson Eggerichs wrote a book in 2004 titled, *Love & Respect.* The premise of his entire book is that a woman's greatest need is to be loved, while a man's greatest need is to be respected.

Dr. Eggerichs asserts that love is spelled C-O-U-P-L-E by the wife. This acronym stands for closeness, openness, understanding, peacemaking, loyalty, and esteem. Conversely, respect is spelled C-H-A-I-R-S by the husband.

This acronym stands for the following words: conquest, hierarchy, authority, insight, relationship, and sexuality.

His extensive research found that how the need for love and the need for respect actively play off of one another in a marriage are foundational to the type of marriage every couple will have. [11]

In short, Dr. Eggerichs asserts that wives want their husbands to be close to them, open up to them, be committed to them, listen, rather than attempt to fix them, facilitate peacemaking by conveying sorrow for hurting them, and to honor and cherish them.

Wouldn't you agree that his recommendations sound like marital vows being said at the marriage alter?

Indeed they do!

So, perhaps meeting our wives needs isn't that complex.

In terms of the key to facilitating and keeping the marital connection, as well as preventing or resolving all marital conflicts, Dr. Eggerichs strongly recommends that husbands should love their wives, while wives should show respect for their husbands.

In his groundbreaking book, *His Needs, Her Needs*, Harley found that wife's marital needs fell into the following 5 categories: conversation, affection, openness and honesty, family commitment, and financial support. [12]

In a research-based book, *The 5 Love Needs of Men and Women*, Dr. Gary and Barbara Rosberg similarly found that a wife's five most important marital needs [13] are:

1. Unconditional love and acceptance

2. Emotional intimacy and communication

3. Spiritual intimacy

4. Encouragement and affirmation

5. Companionship

In my view, a wife's two highest weighted marital needs fall within the two broad categories of connecting communication and affectionate behavior. I discussed the importance of meeting these two marital needs in my book, *The Perfect Marriage*.

Over 90% of the wives I counsel indicate that poor communication is the presenting problem that has prompted the need for couple's counseling.

While I have already indicated that it is my view that poor or dysfunctional communication is the end result of marital needs not being met, to a wife, connecting communication is an end to itself. In this regard, wives simply enjoy communicating for its' own sake, quite similar to men's disposition towards sexual intimacy. To wives, it is the channel to intimacy and the indicator of their husband's interest and them being prioritized.

Husbands often ask me what is meant by the words, *connecting communication*.

In short, the word *connecting* means intimate or very personal, and goes beyond small talk, what happened talk, or chit chat.

Connecting communication is engaging communication.

<u>Elements of Connecting Communication</u>. There must be several elements present for a wife to perceive that marital communication is engaging or positive.

Listed below are the essentials which are required by you, the husband:

- Complete and undivided attention, including direct eye contact.

- Verbal and non-verbal expressions of genuine interest in what she is saying.

- Letting her know that she can openly and safely express what she is thinking and feeling.

- Sincerely attempting to understand what she is saying and feeling.

- Listening carefully, without interrupting or daydreaming.

- Showing respect and unconditional regard for her point-of-view.

- Acknowledging and validating her thoughts and feelings.

- Attempting to enable her to reach a satisfactory closure to the issue(s) she has brought to your attention.

- Showing her that you relate to and appreciate what she has brought to your attention.

- Being verbally supportive, so she hears your support.

To drive home my point with husbands during couples counseling sessions, I challenge them with this question: *In terms of communication, what things would you consider to be appropriate for another man to say to your wife if you were not in the room because these things should only be said by a husband?*

Would you feel that a man crossed the line if he said any of these following statements to your wife: *You're beautiful, I missed you, I think of you all of the time, You're special, You are the best thing that ever happened to me, I really appreciate you, You're the best!*, or *What can I do to make you happy?*

When I present it this way, husbands quickly understand. Do you? Do you get it?!

Husbands, I am sure that you do not have to read a book to know or solicit advice from a friend or professional that your wives need to be romanced as well. And by this time, if you were being attentive, you should know that your wife predominately processes information auditorily. This is why she places such high value on your listening and attention.

Your listening also needs to be combined with acts and gestures of affection throughout the day.

In fact, I recall that one particular research study found that wives needs a minimum of 8 to 12 meaningful affectionate, but non-sexual touches, a day.

Sir, this constitutes a marital need!

Now that you are aware of the importance of this marital need, you have no excuse for not meeting it, regardless of whether she asks for it or not.

To her, having to ask for you to show her that she is special actually takes away from it being special.

Consider how you feel when you have to ask your wife to have sex.

Doesn't something inside you already know that, if this need were valued by her, she would initiate interest on her own?

Therefore, do not forget the formula for making your wife feel loved:

Connecting Communication + Affection = LOVE

Love is Blind! The Story of the Wife Who Nit-Picked

Husbands, I would like to illustrate how the absence of a primary emotional need adversely affects a marital relationship. To do so, I will use a couple that I had an opportunity to work with a number of years ago.

This middle-aged couple came into treatment as a result of the wife's anger towards her husband's "immature and inconsiderate" behavior, according to the wife. The husband was completing his undergraduate degree while she worked full time selling pharmaceuticals. Thus, he spent a great deal of time at home studying. However, while studying, he would be messy and not pick up after himself. His excuse for not doing so was that his wife was a "clean-freak" who expected everything to be in perfect order the moment she arrived home from work.

After several sessions, the husband had made significant and noticeable progress and had an excellent attitude, to match. It then became quite evident that his wife began to nit-pick unjustifiably while continuing to exhibit an attitude that was attached to his old unacceptable behavior. In fact, it appeared that she actually began to create in her mind behaviors and motives for them that he was in no way exhibiting.

The relationship then began to escalate in conflict to a point where his wife was threatening divorce, even though she could not support her reason to any of his past behaviors.

I was puzzled and knew that there was an underlying key issue or relational dynamic that I was apparently missing. At this point, I decided to use my intuition in attempting to ascertain the true nature of this couple's core problem. In doing so, I looked intently upon the wife's countenance and noticed a very frightened, unhappy, and unfulfilled person.

It then intuitively occurred to me to ask her the following question: *Do you feel that your husband loves you?*

At that point, she instantly began crying almost uncontrollably and exclaimed, *No, I don't!*

This was the breakthrough.

At that point, I directed the therapy by having the couple relinquish their defenses and honestly discuss their love for each other. She needed a lot of verbal reassurance.

Her perception of his love was adversely contaminated by a poor relationship in which she was abandoned, coupled with a childhood which was abusive and abandoning by nature.

The fact that her husband would shortly be graduating from college and be less dependent upon her, triggered and ignited old unresolved issues which, in turn, stirred up unresolved lifetime feelings of insecurity, abandonment, uncertainty, and fear. She sought to justify these feelings by labeling his behaviors as *extremely negative*. The unresolved issues contaminated her perception of her husband and the hope for marital happiness. Thus, she perceived herself to be a victim and exhibited behaviors that would ultimately support her negative feelings by making it impossible for her husband to continue to put love into practice and stay in the marriage.

But the breakthrough had been achieved.

With heart, the husband told his wife how he truly felt and was able to convince her that he loved her unconditionally, that she meant everything to him and that he would be with her, *till death do us part.*

The following week, I saw the husband individually because his wife was working out of town. When I inquired as to how the relationship was, the husband chuckled and stated that he has never been so sloppy and negligent around the house --- *but my wife thinks that I am perfect and walk on water!*

The example of this couple supports the notion that *love is blind.* That is, we see in others whom we love and feel loved by what we want to see, and this is based largely upon what is present in our heart toward that person. The result of my therapeutic intervention in this case also supports my contention that marital discord is a symptom of unfulfilled primary emotional needs and that, when one of them is not met, negative emotions get ignited and everything goes hay-wire.

7 Essentials for Connecting With Your Wife

The following are 7 recommendations for you, the husband, to apply in your marriage:

1. **Treat your wife "with royalty."**

Perhaps the greatest gift you can give your wife is to make her feel special by treating her in ways that shows her that she is held in very high regard. To feel special, she needs to be treated in a way that is fitting to a Queen and, in fact, be assured that, in your eyes, no one can match her. In short, she needs to feel highly valued.

In order to show her that she is valued highly, you need to compliment her every day and let her know by your sincere and heartfelt actions that she is deeply loved, appreciated, desired, and very attractive.

2. **Prioritize your wife, by making her feel like she is #1 in your life.**

To put it simply, she must feel that she is #1! Please put your wife first because there is not a woman in the world who will be second to anything or anyone.

Do you hear what I am saying?!

Your wife must feel that she is #1.

I hope that, by this point, you have figured out that a paycheck will simply not be enough for her to feel #1, regardless of your intent.

Your wife knows that you are a hard worker. But she also knows that you would still be a hard worker whether you were married to her or not.

Your wife needs to feel that she takes priority in your heart, mind, and every aspect of your life. She must feel that she comes before your work, goals, family, friends, outside interests, the television, material possessions, finances, sleep, any unfinished business etc.

If your wife does not feel like #1, she will not feel special.

Your wife needs to know that she is in your mind and heart first and foremost.

Believe me, unless she feel #1, she will feel last in your list of priorities.

As a male, I cannot understand why wives tend to feel last if they do not feel first. However, I consistently find this to be the case. They must feel prioritized.

In response to my over-focus in completing my work-related paperwork, I recall my wife commenting that she did not feel like a priority at that moment because, *Joe, if the President of the United States called, you would stop everything you are doing to talk to him!*

Ouch!

A rule of thumb to use in determining whether your wife feels first in your life is to simply ask her, and then to do whatever she requires of you to feel that way.

Your wife must feel like she is #1 in your life, regardless of your intentions or efforts. Thus, you must try harder and do more until this marital need is completely met. There are no short-cuts to meeting this marital need; she determines whether it is or is not met.

Think about all of the time you devote to your work and your interests, such as sports or your hobbies. Do you spend more time on these things than in connecting with her?

This is why it is so important for you and your wife to develop and engage in a common interest together.

If your wife perceives that she is being treated as #1 in your life, she will automatically feel as though she is being treated as a Queen. After all, there is no one higher than a Queen, and a Queen is indeed #1.

Your wife certainly did not say, *I do*, with the thought that she would be second to anything in your life. Also, she turned aside every other man on this planet in her belief that you would not disappoint her. Your wife placed a great deal of faith in you at the marriage alter by placing her whole life and hope for happiness into your hands.

At the marriage alter you were, in effect, crowned as King by your wife.

There is no worthier marital goal than making your wife feel like a Queen. It is essential to her feeling loved.

Wait no longer.

Begin doing it now!

3. Give your wife an adequate amount of marital quality time.

The importance of spending a lot of marital quality time with your wife cannot be over-emphasized. If your wife is special and indeed #1 in your life, you will automatically want to spend as much time with her as possible. This time should be used by you as an opportunity to meet her most important marital needs.

Simply spending time with her cannot necessarily count as quality time unless your wife is getting her marital needs met and perceives the time spent as "quality time."

Have you taken the time to learn what your wife's most important marital needs are?

Please consider the fact that your wife will have less of a need to divert her energies into other things and the children if she feels connected to you. For her to feel connected to you, I would like to emphasize that marital quality time must entail connecting communication and affection in doing things of mutual interest. This, in turn, will make her feel more responsive to your most important needs.

As I hope you can see, there is a reciprocal benefit in spending quality time with your wife.

Remember, quality time means exhibiting quality behavior which is suitable to meet her needs to the fullest degree possible.

The amount of time that is necessary will depend upon whether and when these needs are completely met.

If you are approaching the need for giving your wife sufficient marital quality time with a clock-in, clock-out mentality as you do in work, you need an "attitude adjustment."

Approach meeting your wife's marital needs in the same manner in which you would like her to meet yours. Don't be like children who always have to be reminded.

4. **Give of yourself compassionately to your wife.**

Synonyms for compassion are *giving, sensitivity, tender-heartedness,* and *warm-heartedness.* For these important qualities to be exhibited towards your wife, you will need to make active and ongoing attempts to understand and validate her feelings.

Please understand that a woman and her feelings are one.

Never forget that.

Thus, if you negate or neglect your wife's feelings, she will perceive this as indifference, disregard, rejection, or that do not value her highly. As a result, she will not feel loved by you to the degree she would like and, at a minimum, feel discontented with the marriage. In turn, she will find it very difficult to feel comfortable in responding physically to you.

Can you blame her?

Think about your natural reaction when you feel disrespected. Do you feel like being warm and fuzzy?

Then why would you expect her to feel the same, with respect to your most pressing marital needs?

If you are making attempts to be compassionate to your wife, you will also want to change those habits or behaviors which cause her to experience pain, discomfort, feelings of neglect, or lack of fulfillment.

Do you recall vowing *to cherish and comfort* your wife at the marriage alter? This is what I am talking about.

Moreover, you cannot possibly meet all of your wife's marital needs if you do not understand what they are. In order to truly understand what they are, you must also be able to understand how she feels about them; this cannot occur without a high level of connecting with her.

Lastly, she needs to be able to count on you as someone whom she can lean on, confide in, share with, and feel free to open up to. In other words, she needs you to be her friend, therapist, and patient all wrapped up in one!

5. **Connect with your wife.**

The extreme importance and value of connectedness in every aspect of the marital relationship has been emphasized repeatedly. Connectedness has been referenced within the context of engaging communication. In this regard, your wife needs to feel that you are engaged in the conversation with her with interest and regard for her underlying needs.

For your wife to perceive that communication is positive, you must give her your undivided attention, show positive regard for her views, allow her to be herself, be understanding and patient, be transparent, validate her feelings, relate to her, be reassuring, and be verbally supportive.

Being able to freely and transparently be herself, in terms of talking about anything, while having your heartfelt interest, concern, and undivided attention, is what she needs in a nutshell.

Your wife wants to have the closest and most intimate relationship with you as possible. This should not be perceived as an inconvenience but, rather, an answer to your prayers.

Think about it – isn't this what a marital relationship is supposed to be all about?

Please keep in mind that a starting point for any close relationship is in the mutual sharing of thoughts and feelings, acceptance and understanding of each other's views, and a reciprocal interchange of emotional support.

Remember, it is through the channel of connecting communication that your intent and efforts to promote a loving and mutually-fulfilling marital relationship will be possible.

In the previous chapter, your wife was confronted about all of the things she needs to be doing to make a connection with you. Act in a way that prompts her to be responsive to your needs automatically and genuinely.

In short, be the husband your wife dreams of!

The reciprocity of love applies to you in the same way that it applies to her; you will get what you give in some way or form.

6. **Be affectionate with your wife.**

Loving your wife should be exhibited from you by consistently showering her with affection and romance. While innately you may have less of a need for affection than your wife, this does not change the value, regard, or need she has for it. For her, it is an expression and representation of love she needs ongoingly on a daily basis.

When you neglect your wife in this area, you are failing to meet her vital need for attaining marital happiness. Regardless of the reasons that account for you not meeting this marital need completely (and I'm sure that you have them), the fact remains that this is a primary need for her; thus, it must be met fully to attain a mutually-fulfilling marital relationship.

To your wife, affection is a demonstration of love that shows her that she is valued and cherished. Her need for affection, when met completely, will guard your marital relationship against all of the forces that may have a negative effect upon it, such as a third party, and prompt her to perceive you in a very positive way.

Hopefully, you are not expecting to achieve your marriage miracle with a double standard being applied wherein your wife has to make all of the needed changes on her part, while you only have to make the ones that you choose. If this is your mindset or disposition, you are the one most responsible for keeping your marriage stuck in the mud.

You want respect and to be treated in high regard, right?

You want to be honored as the leader in your home, right?

You want great sex, right?

Well, for God's sake, stop blaming your wife for your shortcomings and give everything you have to give, in order to meet all of your wife's marital needs and to make her as happy as possible!

Most importantly, understand that the purpose of leadership is to benefit those who are following your lead. You cannot be an effective leader sitting on a couch or a rocking chair.

Be honest; do all of your actions, dispositions, and decisions benefit your wife?

Ask your wife what's missing from her perceiving you as an effective leader of the home. In addition, ask her what she believes is missing from you and her attaining a consistent 100% connection.

In fact, solicit her opinions about everything.

To be a good leader, you cannot effectively make decisions without making an assessment of the needs of your family members who are under your protection.

Yes, indeed, your role is to provide and protect.

The word, *protect,* goes well beyond answering the call of a robber attempting to break into your house in the middle of the night. It also denotes, *to serve.* By definition, the words, *to serve,* also mean, *to minister to.*

Incidentally, in the Bible, there is a passage in *Ephesians 5:25* that instructs husbands to *love their wives as Christ loved the Church and gave Himself for it.*

Yet, in *Matthew 20:28,* Jesus qualifies His leadership role as one wherein He has come to the world, *not to be served, but to serve.* Therefore, a primary responsibility for fulfilling your leadership role is to be a servant-leader to your wife and family within the home.

If asked, would your wife say that you are an effective servant leader?

Being an effective servant unquestionably fulfills your high calling for being a leader to your wife and family.

Perhaps, you are not interested in reading about my Biblical interpretation regarding your role as a husband.

Hopefully you are.

If you aren't, however, I would like to make you aware that *spiritual intimacy* was found within the top 5 love needs of wives in extensive marital research conducted by Dr. Gary and Barbara Rosberg.

The Rosberg's research found that spiritual intimacy contained several components for wives, all of which contribute to her security and happiness in your marriage. In this regard, generally speaking, wives want their husbands to be growing spiritually. Moreover, they desire their husbands to be in fellowship with other Christians. Also, they need their husbands to develop and express their spiritual gifts. Lastly, wives need their husbands to be spiritual leaders in the home. [14]

Sir, ask your wife about whether spiritual intimacy is a marital need of hers, and inquire about the weight of this need to her.

If you are not interested in a spiritual perspective or Biblical justification for making various changes as a husband, simply ask your wife what you need to do to completely meet all of her marital needs. I predict that you'll get the same answer; she would like a certain degree of spiritual intimacy.

If you are not interested in what God has to say regarding marriage, why then did you say marital vows, which is a God-ordained and God-instituted act?

When you got married, you "signed-up for marriage," which is a spiritual act. If you are not interested in meeting your wife's need in this area of the marriage, it would appear that you got married in the same way that one signs up for a sport. Therefore, your half-hearted and semi-involved interest in spiritual matters with your wife is similar to practicing a sport at will, as well as picking-and-choosing what drills you will partake in from the directives of your coach.

And when it's game time, you audaciously want to be the first string Quarterback.

Your active involvement in the domestic needs of the home also pertains to the issue of providing and protecting.

Are you a team player in this aspect of marriage?

While I may be conveying a harsh tone, please understand that, like a broken record, I hear wives complain about their husband's lack of domestic support all day-long in my counseling sessions with married couples. While there are exceptions, the majority of wives complain about being left with most or all of the responsibility for attending to the domestics of the house, including the responsibility of making needed repairs.

To fulfill your role as a servant-leader, please make the necessary changes that will make your wife feel cared for and an equal partner in the marriage.

She will admire you for it.

You do want expressed admiration, don't you?

7. **Facilitate oneness with your wife.**

To develop your marriage into a healthy relationship with your wife, you must convey your appreciation of her unique value and attempt to promote her individuality. Building a sense of togetherness and a shared vision of your marriage is a by-product of joining with her in all aspect of your relationship. Therefore, you should never act independently from her, refrain from doing things outside of the marriage that upsets her, involve her in decision-making, and solicit her opinions about everything pertaining to the marriage, including finances.

Are you ready to begin doing these things to your wife's complete satisfaction?

While I realize that you would rather prefer discussing your favorite sport, interest, or hobby than to hear about your wife's day and her feelings, just think about how empty your life would be without her. Perhaps her interests would expand to include your interests if she felt more like a companion and an equal team player in the marriage.

Since your wife is likely to direct much of her attention to the children, you can do much to capture her heart completely by helping her with the challenges they present and, in the spirit of cooperative co-parenting parent, attend to their emotional, developmental, social, educational, and physical needs.

Simply ask your wife about how you can be a better parent and co-parent more effectively with her. I can assure you that she will not pass up the opportunity to tell you, and that she will feel more connected to you for asking.

While men tend to be competitive, goal-oriented, and sexual beings, women tend to be emotional, relational, and spiritual beings. Thus, as a husband, your focus must be along these dimensions to meet her needs for companionship, emotional closeness, and significance. This includes meeting her needs for spiritual leadership in the home.

Your wife also needs to be regularly reassured that your heart is focused on her and whatever you do for her is motivated by your love for her and your heartfelt desire to make her happy, as well. While you may feel that verbalizing your commitment to fidelity to her over and over is being redundant and unnecessary, she will perceive it as reassuring.

Are you willing to be the best spouse as possible and meet all of your wife's stated marital needs completely and without limitations, according to what makes her happiest?

It should take you no longer than 15 seconds or less.

Chapter 8

Keys to Getting Your Marriage Miracle
In 15 Seconds or Less!

This chapter is devoted to the systematic implementation of the marriage miracle recommendations that have been provided herein.

Shift Your Thinking to a Love-Based Mindset

The following mindset changes are recommended necessities for your marriage miracle:

Old Thinking	New Love-Based Thinking
• People don't change and, if they do, it takes years.	Change is only 15 seconds or less away.
• The direction to Florida from New Jersey is Interstate 95 North.	The direction to Florida from New Jersey is Interstate 95 South.
• Love is a feeling and exhibited by simple acts of kindness.	Love is an action involving the gift of giving of oneself for the other person's benefit.

- Love asks, *Why aren't I getting all of my marital needs met?*

  Love asks, *What is it that I need to be saying, doing, or giving to make you as happy as possible?*

- My spouse is the primary problem.

  My negative mindset, arising from my fear and self-focus is the primary problem.

- Exhibiting defensiveness is a product of being mistreated by your spouse.

  Defensiveness is the evidence of your fear, in combination with not be accountable for short-changing your spouse and being focused on yourself, rather than putting 100% love into practice.

- Meeting one or more of my spouse's marital needs is something that I should do if my spouse deserves it, and if and when I feel like it, especially if my spouse has hurt me.

  My spouse is entitled to get his or her marital needs met 100%, and 100% of the time. The basis for these entitlements are the marriage vows of which remain stable throughout time.

- A better and conflict-free marriage is the standard for attaining a happy and mutually-fulfilling marriage.

  The perfect marriage, characterized by putting love into action on a moment-to-moment basis, is the only means to attaining a bona-fide and mutually-fulfilling marriage.

- The word "faithful" applies strictly to marital fidelity.

  The word "faithful" applies to all of the marital vows, as all of the vows are obligations.

- The mindset that says, *My spouse has no right or business in telling me what to do or having any expectations.*

  The mindset that says, "In marriage, *Two have become One*," which means that my spouse and I both have rights and responsibilities to each other because we are married, in accordance with our marriage vows.

- Negotiating and compromising marital needs will be bring peace and reconciliation to the marriage.

  Negotiating and compromising violates the entire letter and spirit of the marriage vows, especially the vow, *To love*, because the intent of negotiating and compromising is to give as little as possible with the intent of getting as much as possible.

- Not permitting your spouse to control you and force you to meet his or her marital needs.

  Adopting a *give what you want to get* mindset.

- Exploring and analyzing the past is the best way of addressing and resolving marital issues.

  The past cannot be changed by a never-ending focus on it. The past should be used as a frame of reference regarding what should not be said or done in the present and future.

- Poor communication or lack of communication represent the primary marital problems.

  Poor communication or a lack of communication in the marriage are symptoms of the problems, arising from unmet marital needs.

Are you ready to make these changes for your marriage miracle? Please say *Yes* in 15 seconds or less! The moment you do, you will be on the right road, headed in the right direction.

You've come this far; please don't turn back now!

Verbalize Your Commitment

Inform your spouse that you are 100% committed to making the necessary changes that will make him or her as happy as possible. Your true commitment will be evident when things do not go as you had planned or hoped.

In reality, your true commitment begins where your motivation ends.

Thus, when you need to be motivated to meet any of your spouse's marital needs, you are not exhibiting bona-fide commitment.

Commitment is evidence of love in practice because it involves sacrificial, as opposed to conditional or contingency-type, giving.

Verbalize your commitment to your spouse, in 15 seconds or less!

Prioritize Your Marriage

Putting anyone, including the children, or anything else before the marriage should be a thing of the past. You did not say marital vows to your children, friends, boss, relatives, parents, associates or anyone else. The one who is failing to ongoingly, consistently, and completely meet the marital needs of his or her spouse is not prioritizing the marriage. You cannot put the marriage first with a mindset of putting yourself or anything or anyone else first while, simultaneously, doing what is necessary to have a strong marriage, only if and when you feel like it.

Will you prioritize your marriage? Please say *Yes* in 15 seconds or less!

Be Present-Focused

You can have the perfect marriage on a moment-by-moment basis as you put love into practice in your marriage on a moment-by-moment basis. Therefore, it is essential that you refrain from discussing the mistakes of the past.

Consider the fact that one who brings up the past is typically focused on themselves and seeking their own highest good, as opposed to their spouse's highest good. Moreover, taking into account wrongs suffered (the antithesis of *love* as, by definition) is most often the focus when the past is brought up in the discussion.

Are you willing to keep your focus and your discussions in the present with your spouse?

Please say *Yes* in 15 seconds or less!

Make an Agreement to Keep Each Other "On Track."

For the stated purpose of protecting and safeguarding the marriage, invite your spouse to bring it to your attention whenever you are giving of yourself less than 100%.

When shortcomings are brought to your attention, thank your spouse and reiterate your commitment to continue at work in making the needed changes that will make him or her completely happy and fulfilled as a spouse.

Are you willing to give and receive constructive and well-meaning feedback in order to stay on track, in terms of what love requires, for a mutually-fulfilling and harmonious marriage?

Please say *Yes* in 15 seconds or less!

Accept Personal Responsibility and Be Accountable

While you may not be responsible for all of the marital problems that exist between you and your spouse, you must accept responsibility for your part. What have you failed to say, do, or give that has contributed to the marital conflict, the marital distress and your spouse's unhappiness? Solicit your spouse's view on this and then make the needed changes.

The following are examples of negative behaviors that you need to change and monitor for attaining *the perfect marriage* with your spouse:

- Lack of a full commitment to your spouse's happiness and highest good.

- Failure to be the type of companion your spouse desires.

- Having a self-centered, judgmental, and critical attitude.

- Giving of yourself to your spouse with limitations and/or conditions (i.e., bartering).

- Acting independently of, as opposed to acting in conjunction with, your spouse.

- Meeting less than 100% of your spouse's stated marital needs.

- Prioritizing work, hobbies, children, others etc. over your spouse and the marriage.

- Being "unfaithful," in terms of fulfilling any of your marital vows.

- Being emotionally, spiritually, or physically indifferent or disengaged from your spouse.

- Refusal to forgive your repentant spouse.

- Failure to make the time necessary to attain a minimum of 15 hours of marital quality time per week with your spouse.

- Acting independently of your spouse in matters pertaining to your marriage.

- Using victimization as an excuse for shortchanging the fulfillment of your spouse's marital needs and/or in exhibiting unacceptable behavior.

- Attempting to negotiate your spouse's marital needs, as opposed to meeting them completely and unconditionally.

- Permitting your marriage to remain in a state of conflict or co-existence.

- Failure to grow emotionally, spiritually, and intellectually with your spouse.

- Acting in a superficial or disconnecting manner with your spouse.

- Failure to do what is necessary to develop balance with your life, in conjunction with your marriage.

- Developing an addiction and permitting it to have an adverse effect in your marriage.

- Failure to establish marital goals and/or do marital ratings with your spouse.

- Failure to change the manner that you communicate with your spouse, as has been recommended herein.

- Making changes in a hit-or-miss fashion, wherein you give up trying in response to not getting the exact and immediate results that you would like.

Are you willing accept personal responsibility and be accountable, as recommended herein?

Please say *Yes* in 15 seconds or less!

Be Reciprocally-Supportive

Anything that thwarts or impedes marital love should be discussed immediately in the spirit of protecting the relationship. Encouragement, providing comfort, being receptive to your spouse's feedback, the willingness to listen, and being quick to point out progress that has been made are all essential for conveying support and making relationship progress.

Are you willing to be supportive to your spouse?

Please say *Yes* in 15 seconds or less!

Forgive

Love spells G-I-V-E. The last 4 letters of the word forgive spells G-I-V-E.

For love to be legitimately given, forgiveness is essential… and it should be given in 15 seconds or less! Unforgiveness takes wrongs into account, which is the antithesis of love.

In choosing to forgive, you will refrain from bringing up the past and also holding past mistakes and shortcomings against your spouse. Deliberately refusing to forgive your repentant spouse is a conscious, willful, and deliberate wrongdoing that will poison any attempts for a marital transformation.

You will also stop focusing on your victimization but, rather, seek to say, do, or give whatever will be in your spouse's best interests.

It should be noted that forgiveness is an event, whereas rebuilding trust is a process. Thus, it will take time to heal and rebuild trust. The positive changes you make, in conjunction with your consistency, will be instrumental in rebuilding the trust.

Are you willing to forgive your spouse for all of your spouse's wrongdoings?

Please say *Yes* in 15 seconds or less!

Give What You Want to Get

Be willing to resist the temptation to respond or reciprocate in a negative way to mean-spirited comments that are directed towards you. Reacting defensively to non-loving words and actions is like putting more dark laundry into the white laundry rather than whitener. In short, give what you want to get.

Are you willing to practice the Golden Rule, by treating your spouse in the way that you wish to be treated?

Please say *Yes* in 15 seconds or less!

Put "The Magic Formula" Into Effect

The Magic Formula for attaining *the perfect marriage* contains 3 essential components:

1. Develop a love mindset that always and unconditionally asks the question, *What it is that I need to be saying, doing, or giving in order to please my spouse completely?* This requires that you refrain from becoming upset about what you are not getting from your spouse.

2. Make a commitment to completely and consistently meet all of your spouse's marital needs to his/her complete satisfaction.

3. Obtain a minimum of 15 hours of marital quality time per week, with a focus on developing intimacy, having fun, and fulfilling each other's need for marital companionship.

Are you willing to consistently meet all of your spouse's marital needs unconditionally and exhibit this commitment by spending no less than 15 hours of marital quality time a week with your spouse?

Please say *Yes* in 15 seconds or less!

Write a List of Your Primary Marital Needs to Specification

You and your spouse should specify in writing what your marital needs are and what it will take to meet them completely. The giver is responsible for meeting the receiver's marital needs to the receiver's specification.

Some examples of marital needs are as follows:

- Marital quality time (intimacy, fun, and companionship time spent together).

- Connecting communication.

- Affection.
- Engaging in growth-oriented activities.
- Having deep and meaningful conversations.
- Going to church together.
- Consistently fulfilling, in letter and spirit, all of your marriage vows.
- Making marital decisions together.
- Domestic support.
- Working as a team in raising the children.
- Engaging in social and recreational activities together.
- Developing and practicing common interests.
- Sexual fulfillment.
- Establishing a mutual and congruent vision for the marriage.
- Finding a balance between work, rearing of the children, rest, and prioritizing the marriage.
- Making each other appealing and attractive to each other.
- Exhibiting reciprocal love and respect.
- Establishing and working on marital goals.

Are you willing to meet all of your spouse's marital needs, to your spouse's specification, regardless of your motivation, preference, energy level, other obligations etc.?

Please say *Yes* in 15 seconds or less!

Complete Marital Ratings for Progress Checks Twice a Week

After writing out your list of marital needs and the specific desired changes you would like your spouse to make to meet them completely, assign ratings from 0-10, to represent the degree to which your spouse is meeting each one of them to your degree of satisfaction.

You may use the following rating key as a guideline for your ratings:

A rating from "**0-3**" represents getting your marital need met <u>rarely to minimally</u>.

A rating from "**4-6**" represents getting your marital need <u>met at times or inconsistently</u>.

A rating from "**7-9**" represents getting your marital need met from the degree of
<u>generally to most often</u>.

A rating of "**10**" represents that your spouse is meeting your marital need <u>to your</u>
<u>complete satisfaction</u>.

Please note on the following page an example of how to do a marital rating regarding one particular marital need, based upon a stated marital need of achieving a greater degree of connecting communication.

Marital Ratings for Charting Progress

<u>Rating Key</u>: **0-3 (Rarely-Minimally); 4-6 (At times, inconsistently); 7-9 (Generally-Most Often); 10 (To my complete satisfaction)**

<u>Marital Needs:</u>

1. To achieve a greater degree of connecting communication.

Desired changes from my spouse (to attain a "10" rating to meet this need completely):

- To keep the tone of the conversation at a normal level.
- To refrain from using foul language during our discussions.
- To not become defensive to anything that I choose to bring to my spouse's attention.
- To not interrupt me until I have finished talking.
- To show respect and consideration for my feelings and opinions.
- To be open, honest, and transparent when discussing sensitive and personal topics.

- To be non-critical and non-judgmental regarding anything I have said.

<u>Your Ratings of Your Spouse</u> (<u>regarding the need to achieve greater connecting communication):</u>

1st Rating of the week (Wed.): 3 (minimally)
2nd Rating of the week (Sat.): 8 (most often)
3rd Rating (Next Wed): A number will be chosen from the *Rating Key* on the previous page.

<u>Note</u>: These marital ratings are to be completed (for each of your stated marital needs) at least 2 times per week, of the two days of your choosing. Each of you are to share your ratings with each other and specify why the rating was given and what is needed to bring the rating to a "10." You and your spouse should keep a log of your ratings to track progress. Each of you may list as many marital needs as you wish. It is advisable to agree about the day and time for the review of your ratings. If 100% love is being practiced, both of you should bring your ratings from where they are to a "10" in very little time. The ratings are a means of providing each other with feedback so each of you know exactly what the other needs to say, do, or give to bring each rating to a "10," which represents having that need met to complete satisfaction.

Are you willing to track your progress with your spouse on a regular basis?

Please say *Yes* in 15 seconds or less!

Attempt to Exceed Your Spouse's Degree of Complete Satisfaction

If at all possible, meet your spouse's need to a rating of an "11," especially if it is a primary marital need.

In this regard, attempt to exceed what would be totally satisfactory to your spouse. For example, if your spouse would like 3 kisses a day, give him/her 4 kisses.

If your spouse would like to go out on a date at least 1 time a month, attempt to squeeze in another date.

If your spouse requires 20 hours of marital quality time a week, give him/her 21 hours.

Are you willing to meet your spouse's marital needs in excess to what his or her stated degree of satisfaction?

Please say *Yes* in 15 seconds or less!

Maximizing Marital Quality Time

Your marriage miracle is only within reach to the degree that you get a <u>minimum</u> of 15 hours of marital quality time together.

While this is one of the most important recommendations for attaining a mutually-fulfilling marriage, it is the most ignored or resisted. Simply being alone together is not enough!

An adequate amount of marital quality time is essential for a quality marriage. It is the time spent together which results in marital needs being met. And to reiterate what was emphasized in Chapter 3, *you will never find the time if you do not make the time.*

If you are committed to your spouse's happiness, you will maximize marital quality time.

Do you work during the day, while your spouse works at night? If this is the case, you both will have to spend every spare moment with each other or play *catch up* during the weekend. *Where there's a will, there's a way* applies here.

Remember, marital quality time does <u>not</u> have to involve the spending of money. You can be obtaining marital quality time while eating dinner together or watching the same t.v. show that you both enjoy.

Mutual agreement in what constitutes "marital quality time" between you and your spouse is essential.

You can also fit in small doses of marital quality time throughout the day, such as calling each other a few times or more throughout the day. Moreover, you can write endearing letters to each other if your work schedule conflicts with each other.

Any of the home-related responsibilities can be used to obtain marital quality time if there is a sense that you are working together as a team and formulating decisions together or working in conjunction with each other.

Going out to a small and inexpensive lunch or dinner once or twice a week can also be a connecting experience. Please be careful that you do not use this precious time to engage in complaining or a discussion of matters that simply create tension or conflicts between you.

Are you willing to spend a maximum amount of marital quality time on a continuous basis with your spouse?

Please say *Yes* in 15 seconds or less!

Replace Objections With Solutions

Reaching a marital consensus is okay, as long as it is not perceived as "compromising, or not involve shortchanging your spouse from getting 100% of his or her marital needs met.

To put love into actual practice in your marriage, each of you should be more interested in the happiness of the other. In attempting to make each other happy, you may reach an impasse with respect to making a decision at times. For example, your husband may ask you where you would like to go out on a date. In this regard, you may wish to visit relatives, whereas he may wish to go out to dinner.

If you both show equal regard for the other's wishes, you should be able to make a mutually-satisfactory decision together. Using the example above, perhaps you and your husband could go to dinner earlier in the evening and then visit your relatives afterward.

In other matters pursuant to the issue of attempting to reach a consensus, a *rule of thumb* that should be applied is that the spouse with the complaint or objection to a particular suggestion must come up with a proposed solution after his or her objection.

If, in turn, your spouse disagrees with what you have presented as an alternative option, you must then provide your proposed solution in response to your objection.

Ultimately, you and your spouse must arrive at a mutually-agreeable solution with each other's marital needs and highest good in mind. Therefore, in matters of disagreement regarding decisions, be careful not to shortchange any of your spouse's marital needs.

Are you willing to stop insisting on having your own way but, instead, agree to engage in a dialogue with your spouse?

Are you willing to discuss matters of disagreement with your spouse until you both reach a harmonious consensus with your spouse regarding matters of disagreement?

In matters of disagreement regarding matters involving decision-making, are you willing to not use your different point-of-view to shortchange any of your spouse's marital needs?

Please say *Yes* in 15 seconds or less!

How to Distribute Your Energy in Meeting Your Spouse's Primary Marital Needs

To WIVES

50% of your success in being the wife of your husband's dreams will be attributed to meeting your husband's need for admiration.

Examples of "expressed admiration" include the following: Making positive comments to him and pointing our his positive behaviors and traits; not offering him unsolicited advice of suggestions, regardless of your well-meaning intent; supporting his attempts to set household rules and consequences with the children, refraining from bring up his past or present shortcomings; not complaining; treating him in a manner fitting to a King; being non-defensive; exhibiting respect and high regard for his marital needs; focusing on recreational activities and topics that interest him the most; having an attitude and disposition that conveys the, "Capture Effect;" and desire to prioritize his marital needs completely, "with heart," and a sense of urgency.

35% of your success in being the wife of your husband's dreams will be attributed to meeting your husband's need for sexual fulfillment.

Note: The quantity and quality of sex are applicable, leading to a complete fulfillment of his sexual needs, in terms of what it takes to make him the happiest and satisfy him completely.

15% of your success in being the wife of your husband's dreams will be attributed to meeting the remaining needs of your husband, including domestic support (e.g., cooking, cleaning, raising the children etc.).

In conclusion, <u>your husband's perfect marriage formula is as follows</u>:

<u>EXPRESSED ADMIRATION</u> + <u>SEXUAL FULFILLMENT</u> + <u>DOMESTIC SUPPORT ETC.</u>
(50%) **(35%)** **(15%) = 100%**

100% = **Your Marriage Miracle!**

<u>Note:</u> Most wives spend 85% of their time and energy, devoted to the 15% of what makes a husband happy (i.e., domestic support), and 15% on the remaining 85% of what makes him happy (e.g., admiration and sexual fulfillment).

At this point, you may be saying to yourself, *Does being an excellent wife boil down to giving a husband admiration and meeting his needs for sexual fulfillment?*

Pretty much so.

But you knew that anyway, didn't you?

So, at this point, why are you feeling surprised to any degree?

Please recall the exercise you took wherein you (as well as thousands of other wives) admitted that you would focus on admiration and sexual fulfillment to capture your husband's heart if, by midnight, the lives of your most loved ones depended upon it if he didn't feel 100% connected to you.

Your attitude should be changed at this point from, *Oh, No!* to, *Alright; I'm going for it!*

The manner in which you should approach meeting your husband's primary needs can be depicted by a wife who looks her husband in the eyes and with heartfelt sincerity and passion says, *I'll do anything to please you!*

If you say this to your husband, watch his reaction and then count to 15. Before you reach number 15, he will reciprocate and say the same thing to you.

You will get what you give!

The transforming power of your expressed admiration is literally mind-boggling, yet quite simple to implement.

A husband's need for your expressed admiration is the driving force that unleashes everything he has to offer in order to please you, as well as the key to his growth and development as a person and husband.

As was stated earlier in this book, a husband is basically no different in God in that, without faith, it is impossible to please him.

In the same way that faith unleashes all that God has to offer, as well as He would truly like to give His creation, expressed admiration prompts this same response in a husband.

"A WALK TO REMEMEBER" = A MIRACLE TO BELIEVE IN!

Please recall the movie, *A Walk to Remember*. In this movie, Landon Carter, a cocky, self-centered and defiant 12th grade "bad-boy," whose real struggles are rooted in and linked to unresolved issues regarding his father who abandoned his mother, is forced to help disadvantaged students in school on the weekends and assume the leading role in the school play.

Together, these suspension-related consequences result in Landon spending time with the school nerd and laughing stock, Jamie Sullivan (played by Mandy Moore).

As the movie progresses, Landon progressively falls in love with Jamie, despite the negative opposition he faces from his friends and the school as a whole. Landon's transformation can be best depicted in a scene wherein he is conversing with his mother, who has just brought to his attention that she found a piece of paper that he had written on, wherein he indicated that one of his goals was to get into medical school.

Landon's mother also expressed concern about his involvement with Jamie, in response to Landon just spending the night with her in the woods, wherein they were platonically connecting with each other and viewing the stars through Jamie's telescope. Landon's mother's primary concern was rooted in the fact that Jamie was the Pastor's daughter in their little town.

Landon responds to his mother's concern, coupled with his goal to get into medical school, in a way that totally supports the premise of this book. In this regard, Landon exclaims the following: *Jamie has faith in me. She makes me want to be different, better!*

Despite the fact that Landon ultimately found out that Jamie was dying of Leukemia, he focused all of his attention in meeting her needs. In addition, he proposed to her and they were married the summer after graduation from high school. Shortly thereafter, Jamie died.

At the very end of the movie, Landon visits Jamie's father, and informs him that he was accepted into medical school. This great news became momentarily diminished when Landon suddenly expressed sorrow and regret to Jamie's father that she had not "gotten her miracle."

Earlier in the film, Jamie had shared with Landon the list of her desires, such as getting a tattoo, being in two places at once, getting married in the church where her mother got married, and so forth. Written in her School Yearbook was Jamie's lifetime goal of "witnessing a miracle."

Landon was instrumental in making sure that Jamie's desires or better said, *fantasies*, were fulfilled during their courting. However, Landon conveyed his sorrow that Jamie had died before witnessing a miracle. In this regard, he said to Jamie's father, *I'm sorry that Jamie never got to witness her miracle.*

In response, her father replied, *Yes she did; it was you!*

Yes, indeed, Jamie witnessed the miracle of the transformation of Landon from a self-serving, rude, defiant, and inconsiderate person to a loving and compassionate husband who was on the road to fulfilling the dream of becoming a medical doctor. This dream had become crystallized as a result of Jamie's belief and exhibited faith in him during their courting, and despite the fact that he would have nothing to do with his father, who was a medical doctor.

Jamie indeed witnessed a miracle, and this miracle occurred as a result of her expressed admiration.

And, like the "couple with the sticky floor," she did not have to give him sex to mold him into the man of her dreams.

Like Jamie, your marriage miracle is within your reach.

Take 15 seconds or less; reach out and receive your miracle!

To HUSBANDS

50% of your success in being the husband of your wife's dreams will be attributed to meeting her need for connecting communication.

<u>Examples of connecting communication include the following:</u>

- Open, honest, deep, and transparent discussions;
- Providing her with encouragement, affirmation, understanding, romance, and reassurance;
- Active and engaging listening;
- Validating her and her points-of-view;
- Treating her in a way that conveys to her that she is the number one priority in your life.

<u>LEARN HER LOVE LANGUAGE</u>. You can determine and learn about your wife's love language (as well as yours) by taking a *Love Languages Test* that can be found at: **www.afo.net/hftw-lovetest.asp.**

35% of your success in being the husband of your wife's dreams will be attributed to meeting her need for love and affection, and being emotionally and spiritually intimate with her.

15% of your success in being the husband of your wife's dreams will be attributed to the remainder of her needs, such as leadership, commitment to the family, and giving her an adequate amount of marital quality time.

TABULATING YOUR MARRIAGE MIRACLE

100% Connecting Communication

+

100% Affectionate Behavior

+

100% Commitment to Meeting Her Specific Needs

= Your Marriage Miracle!

Note: Ask your wife to assign a weight value for each of her marital needs so you will know where to focus most of your attention and energy.

Your New Marital Commitment For a New Marital Beginning

As a means of recapping everything that has been recommended herein, are you willing to do the following that has been recommended below? Yes or No?

1. Shift your self-focused thinking to love-based thinking.

2. Verbalize your commitment to completely put love into action in your marriage.

3. Disregard all of the misconceptions about putting love into practice by others who advocate or promote the giving of less than 100% love in a marriage.

4. Stop being controlled by all forms of fear that have a negative impact upon the marriage and does not conform to love, such as defensiveness, engaging in marital power struggles etc.

5. Do an exhaustive search and inquiry to discover or learn more about what pleases your spouse to the greatest degree.

6. Learn your spouse's love language (e.g., acts of service, words of affirmation, gifts, physical touch, quality time) and the weight of each marital need.

7. Give of yourself unconditionally and completely with the goal of meeting all of your spouse's marital needs and making him/her as happy as you possibly can.

8. Prioritize your marriage over everything else, including your job, your interests and hobbies, your children, your parents or anyone else.

9. Be present-focused, as opposed to focused on and bringing up the past.

10. Make an agreement with your spouse to protect and safeguard the marriage by keeping each other on track by bringing non-loved-based shortcomings to each other's attention?

11. Accept responsibility for your part in the past and present marital problems, change your negative behaviors and stop being a victim?

12. Be supportive to your spouse, by comforting, encouraging, being receptive to feedback, willing to listen, and quick to point out marital progress that has been made.

13. Forgive yourself and your spouse.

14. Give to your spouse what you want to get from your spouse.

15. Put *The Magic Formula* into effect.

16. Write a list of your specific primary marital needs and agree to read and meet the marital needs on your spouse's list.

17. Complete marital ratings for progress checks at least twice a week.

18. Attempt to exceed your spouse's degree of complete satisfaction.

19. Maximize marital quality time.

20. Replace your objections with solutions to you and your spouse reach a mutual agreement.

Your Marriage Miracle in 15 Seconds or Less!

Are you ready for your marriage miracle?

You can have one, simply based upon your decision.

For once and for all, kick fear to the curb and resist everything you have heard, read, or been taught that has robbed you of having the marriage of your dreams – a 100% marriage that is completely fulfilling to you and your spouse.

Remember, love never fails!

You now have all of the information you need to have the mutually-fulfilling marriage of your dreams.

Take 15 seconds or less to decide if you will give 100% love a 100% try. You have absolutely nothing to lose, but a 100% marriage to gain.

You will indeed get what you give.

You have nothing to lose and a marriage miracle - *the perfect marriage,* to gain.

The perfect marriage you have desired and struggled to attain is now within your reach.

Say, *Yes!*

Notes

Chapter 1

1. www.aamft.org
2. Wayne W. Dyer, Ph.D., *Your Sacred Self* (New York: Harper Collins, 1995), 242.

Chapter 3

3. Hannah Whitall Smith, *The Christian's Secret Of A Happy Life* (Uhrichsville: Barbour and Company, Inc., 1985), 36.

Chapter 4

4. Gary Chapman, *The Five Love Languages* (Chicago: Northfield Publishing, 2004).

Chapter 6

5. Joseph Racite, Ph.D., *The Perfect Marriage*, (California: "You Deserve It" Creations, 1999), 146.
6. John Gottman, Ph.D., *The Seven Principles For Making Marriage Work*, (New York: Three Rivers Press, 1999), 61-77.
7. Gottman, J.M. & Krokoff, L.J. (1989). *Marital interaction and satisfaction: A longitudinal view.* Journal of Consulting and Clinical Psychology, 57, 47-52.

8. John Gottman, Ph.D., *The Seven Principles For Making Marriage Work*, (New York: Three Rivers Proess, 1999), 115.

9. Joseph Racite, Ph.D., *The Perfect Marriage*, (California: "You Deserve It" Creations, 1999), 160-163.

Chapter 7

10. John Gottman, Ph.D., *Why Marriages Succeed Or Fail*, (New York: Harper Collins Publishers, 1994), 61.

11. Emerson Eggerichs, *Love & Respect*, (Nashville: Thomas Nelson, Inc., 2004)

12. William F. Harley, Jr. *His Needs, Her Needs: Building An Affair-Proof Marriage* (Old Tappen: Fleming H. Revell Co., 1986), 10.

13. Gary & Barbara Rosberg, *The 5 Love Needs of Men & Women* (Wheaton: Tyndale House Publishers, Inc., 2000).

14. Ibid., 122-141.

About the Author

Dr. Joseph Racite is a *Licensed Professional Counselor, Certified Clinical Mental Health Counselor, Nationally Certified Psychologist,* and author of, *The Perfect Marriage.* He has an earned *Ph.D. in Human Services,* with a concentration and *Certificate in Marriage and Family Services.* He has also earned a *Masters Degree* and *Certificate of Advanced Study in Clinical Psychology* from Loyola College. As a therapist for over 33 years, Dr. Racite has helped numerous married couples with his counseling approach, and has been very effective in circumventing divorce and maximizing marriages. For the past 21 years, he has worked in private practice at *Family & Psychological Services, Inc.,* located in Cherry Hill, New Jersey.

Dr. Racite is also Founder and President of *Perfect Marriage Ministries, Inc.* He and his wife, Mary, conduct "Perfect Marriage Seminars," using the principles contained in this book. They are currently involved in the building of a church in Webeye, Kenya, and in also meeting the special needs of this community.